Lesbians and Gay Men: Chemical Dependency Treatment Issues

Lesbians and Gay Men: Chemical Dependency Treatment Issues

Dava L. Weinstein, MSW
Editor

Lesbians and Gay Men: Chemical Dependency Treatment Issues, edited by Dava L. Weinstein, MSW, was simultaneously issued by The Haworth Press, Inc., under the same title, as a special issue of *Journal of Chemical Dependency Treatment*, Volume 5, Number 1 1992, Dana Finnegan, PhD, journal editor.

Harrington Park Press
An Imprint of
The Haworth Press, Inc.
New York • London • Norwood (Australia)

ISBN 1-56023-036-3

Published by

Harrington Park Press, 10 Alice Street, Binghamton, NY 13904-1580

Harrington Park Press is an imprint of The Haworth Press, Inc., 10 Alice Street, Binghamton, NY 13904-1580 USA.

Lesbians and Gay Men: Chemical Dependency Treatment Issues has also been published as *Journal of Chemical Dependency Treatment*, Volume 5, Number 1 1992.

Library of Congress Cataloging-in-Publication Data

Lesbians and gay men : chemical dependency treatment issues / Dava L. Weinstein, editor
      p. cm.
  Also published as Journal of chemical dependency treatment, Vol. 5, no. 1, 1992
  Simultaneously published by the Harrington Park Press.
  Includes bibliographical references.
  ISBN 1-56024-393-7(Haworth : alk. paper).–ISBN 1-56023-036-3(Harrington Park Press : alk. paper)
    1. Gays–Substance use. 2. Substance abuse–Treatment. 3. Substance abuse–Treatment–Social aspects. I. Weinstein, Dava L.
RC564.5.G39L47 1992
616.86'008'664–dc20   92-31975
                                                          CIP

Dedication

Homophobia is a state of fear and fear is a killer. This volume is dedicated to those who have been broken by fear and those who have gone beyond it.

ABOUT THE EDITOR

Dava L. Weinstein, MSW, ACSW is a New York State certified social worker. She has a counseling practice for individuals, couples, and families which focuses on addictions, gay and lesbian counseling, and hypnotherapy. She has authored various professional articles. Dava is particularly interested in the use of family therapy concepts and brief strategic treatment. She has been a member of various professional committees including the New York City Chapter of the National Association of Social Workers Committee on Alcoholism and Other Chemical Dependencies and the Planning Committee of the annual conference, *10% of Those We Serve: Treatment of Alcoholism and Other Addictions Among Gay Men and Lesbians.* Her most recent professional commitment is as a member of the Gay and Lesbian Family Project at the Ackerman Institute for Family Therapy.

CONTENTS

Preface

"Help them, help them, support them," a cry to professionals from a lesbian subject in McNally's study of lesbian recovering alcoholics serves as a subtext for this excellent collection of articles edited by Dava Weinstein which focuses on chemical dependency treatment issues in lesbians and gay men. The emphasis throughout is on the practical methods of delivering that sorely needed help and support. Clinicians working with chemically dependent clients too often have great good will, some superficial understanding of lesbian and gay issues but little concrete information on how and when to approach these issues in the context of addiction treatment. This collection goes far in providing both a comprehensive background for deepening that understanding and gaining some really useful clinical tools. From identifying homophobia in oneself and one's clients to planning an experiential weekend workshop for lesbians and gay men, there is a wide variety of information presented of great use to professionals of all disciplines and any sexual orientation.

Anne Geller, MD
Chief
Smithers Alcoholism Treatment and Training Center
St. Luke's-Roosevelt Hospital Center, New York City

Introduction

This collection of articles is a direct result of a New York City area annual Conference, "10% of Those We Serve, Treatment of Alcoholism and Other Addictions Among Gays and Lesbians." The Conference, first held in 1986, is planned each year by professionals who represent a wide range of organizations and share a common interest in furthering education of health care providers who work with lesbian and gay male clients. Over the years, the Conference has served a number of functions: it provides an opportunity for clinicians to increase their skills in delivery of services to their lesbian and gay clients; an opportunity for lesbian and gay providers to address clinical issues particular to their experience (e.g., boundary issues between provider and client in the overlapping worlds of treatment, social life and self-help movements; being "out" on the job, etc.); and, an opportunity for all the participants to learn about resources available for lesbian and gay clients.

The articles are a continuation of the Conference goal of increasing the health provider's skills. They are by no means inclusive of all areas that need to be addressed. They do, however, make a valuable contribution to the new and growing body of clinical literature about lesbian and gay male mental health issues. The reader is urged to keep bisexual clients in mind as well. Many of the gay and lesbian mental health issues apply to the bisexual experience especially homophobia and all it's attendant problems. As the editor and as a social worker, I am particularly pleased by the clinical focus on the articles. I believe that presentations of theory, case examples and specific clinical techniques will indeed enhance the reader's abilities in his/her clinical practice.

The lead article by Heyward addresses alienation, heterosexism, homophobia and addictions as both social and individual in nature.

Just as her 1989 keynote address to Conference participants created a context for professional learning that day so does this article create the context for the ones that follow. Ubell and Sumberg provide a thoughtful piece on heterosexual therapists treating homosexual addicted clients. Case material and specific recommendations to the reader make the article very useful. Shernoff and Springer raise the issues of working with clients who are both substance abusers and have AIDS. The article focuses on the impact on professionals. Both of these papers address transferential issues between therapist and client.

Kus's specific recommendations for clinicians working with gay men in 12-step programs is based on his research of that population. His exploration of spirituality in everyday life sensitizes the reader to an often overlooked strength. Shifrin and Solis's article on working with lesbian and gay male adolescents focuses attention on substance abuse prevention, gay and lesbian youth in straight service settings, and the role of the family in treatment. They give specific suggestions to school and agency staffs on promoting healthy homosexual identity formation.

Rothberg and Kidder offer a significant contribution to the literature by discussing the interplay between established concepts of roles in alcoholic families and the coming out process of young lesbians. The article then presents implications for treatment and clinical interventions. McNally and Finnegan's article presents McNally's construct of the stages of lesbian recovering alcoholic identity transformation. They then discuss its significance in the treatment of recovering lesbians.

Hellman's guidelines for working with the mentally ill chemically dependent lesbian or gay individual include assessment of mental illness and addiction and assessment of the difference between paranoid ideation secondary to psychosis and appropriate anxiety of homosexuals in a heterosexual society. Picucci's description of an experimental weekend workshop for lesbians and gay men in recovery is sufficiently detailed that it stands on its own as a manual for group facilitators. Weinstein's article makes a case for including three generational family of origin assessment in work with lesbian and gay clients. Specific techniques from the family therapy field are presented as tools for the addiction specialist.

There remain so many areas that have yet to be addressed in the addictions literature about lesbian and gay clients. For example, issues concerning gays and lesbians of color is a large gap. The 10% Conference Committee is striving to address that gap in the 1992 Conference by focusing on alienation, stigma, and difference which lesbian and gay minority persons must deal with in recovery. My hope is that the annual Conference and this collection of articles will encourage clinicians who have developed particular expertise about issues needing discussion to share that knowledge through professional writing.

Finally it is with gratitude that I acknowledge those who made this volume possible. Dana Finnegan, editor of the *Journal of Chemical Dependency Treatment*, has given me invaluable guidance in seeing this project through to fruition. Dorothy Calvani, my life mate, has given me unending support and encouragement.

Dava Weinstein
New York, NY

Healing Addiction and Homophobia: Reflections on Empowerment and Liberation

Carter Heyward, PhD

Let me be clear at the outset that I am *not* simply a feminist liberation theologian or an Episcopal priest who happens to be interested in issues of sexuality and addiction! I am these things, to be sure, but I am also a lesbian who is recovering from alcoholism and bulimia. With other liberation theologians, I believe that the naming of our personal "investments" in the issues on which we are working is essential to honest, ethical, professional engagement.

In this essay, I will suggest some connections between the force of homophobia in our lives and the problem of addiction. I experience, and understand, these connections in the context of a social order characterized by alienation, a massive social dis-order, or disease, which is our common lot in an advanced patriarchal capitalist society.

We are an alienated people. (Fromm, 1961; Heyward, 1989, a,b.) This is a condition of our lives, whether we are lesbian, gay, bisexual, or heterosexual; sexually active or celibate; addicted or not; mental health professionals, priests, teachers, patients, clients, or students. So my first aim in these pages is to explore briefly, in the social context of alienation, some connections between addic-

---

Carter Heyward is Professor of Theology at Episcopal Divinity School in Cambridge, MA.

This article is an adaptation of the address at the "10% of Those We Serve: Treatment of Alcoholism and Other Addictions Among Gays and Lesbians" Conference, April 1989.

5

tion and, especially for those of us who are gay or lesbian, the force of homophobia in our lives.

My second aim is to speak, in this context, of healing and empowerment in my own life-journey to this point. I will be speaking of *healing as empowerment*, critical in the work of liberation from emotionally deadening, spiritually savaging, and physically debilitating social structures of isolation that contribute to, and exacerbate, addiction.

The problems of isolation and addiction are rooted, I am persuaded, in the fear of our radically mutual connectedness with one another, a fear bred and cultivated in such structures of alienation as sexism, heterosexism, racism, able-bodyism, ageism, and classism. In speaking of my participation in the 12-Step program, I will reflect on the life-affirming, healing dimensions of this remarkable resource, and I also will cite certain of its limitations as a resource for healing.

AN ALIENATED PEOPLE

Alienation is not, at root, a feeling.[1] In fact, frequently we do not *feel* alienated at all, which is part of the problem. We learn not to feel, not to see, not to recognize our alienation from one another. But alienation does to our relationships and self-images much what polluted air does to our bodies: it wears us down and, over time, destroys us. So what is it, this alienation?

In a profit-consumed economic order, the value of persons is diminished (Heyward, 1989 a,b). The accumulation of capital on the part of the wealthy and the hope for wealth on the part of the rest of us are designed to take precedence over the essentially non-monetary value of human beings and other earth-creatures as significant and worthy simply because we are who we are. In this context, the capacity to love and respect our bodies, enjoy a strong

---

[1] These sections, "an alienated people" and "heterosexism and homophobia" are excerpted and adapted from *Touching Our Strength* by Carter Heyward. Copyright © 1989 by Carter Heyward. Used with permission from Harper San Francisco, A Division of Harper Collins Publishers.

sense of self-esteem, take real pleasure in our work, and respect and enjoy others, is a weakened capacity. In a literal sense, we have lost ourselves as a people in solidarity with one another and other creatures.

This loss of ourselves and one another is what Karl Marx meant by "alienation." It forms the basis for what Jean Baker Miller names as our "disconnections"-the "intensely confounded opposites of the 'good things' that flow from growth-enhancing, mutually empowering connections" (Miller, 1988). In an alienated situation, no one relates as humanely as she or he might desire. It is not that we do not want to be caring people, nor that we do not want to experience and share the "good things" that flow from mutually empowering relationships. It is, rather, that largely unbeknownst to us in the course of living our daily lives, we are captive to social forces that are in control of our lives, including our feelings and our values.

In this situation of alienation from ourselves and one another, power has come to mean power-over others as well as over our own base "natures." Power has come to mean the domination, however benign, by a few over the lives and deaths of many. I am referring to the real, daily, control of all human and other natural resources: the food we eat, the air we breathe, the energy we burn, the love we make, even the dreams we nurture, are controlled to a large extent by the structural configurations of power which have been shaped by the interests of affluent white males who usually fail to see the exploitative character of their own lives.

The alienation in our life together is so pervasive that we assume it is "natural" and "normal." We assume it is only "natural" to want to come out on top . . . to pull ourselves up by our own bootstraps . . . to distinguish ourselves as better than, other than, separate from. Thus, we learn to live over/against one another, out of touch with the sacred value of that which is most fully human-common-among us. It is important that we see the extent to which our acceptance of alienation as "just the way it is" characterizes our common life in the United States in the late 20th century. This resignation generates a sense of powerlessness among us in which we are largely out of touch with our power-as-a-people to create, to change, and to hope. For, while alienated power is not shared, alienated powerlessness is–and it moves us toward our undoing as a people and a planet. This is the context in which both homophobia and addiction need to be understood for each, in its own way, is a manifestation of alienation.

HETEROSEXISM AND HOMOPHOBIA

Homophobia cannot be understood adequately as simply the fear of same-sex love, although linguistically this is its Greek etiology. No one is born homophobic. No one is born erotophobic either, afraid of our erotic power to connect with one another, which is also our sacred power for creativity and liberation (Heyward, 1989, a, b). Homophobia can be understood adequately only insofar as we see that its origins are not "in" us, as if we were separate monad-like characters inflicted with a strange disease. Homophobia's roots are in social structures of alienation which shape our lives, including our psyches. In particular, homophobia is rooted in the structure of heterosexism, the basic structure of gay/lesbian oppression in this and other societies.

Heterosexism is to homophobia what sexism is to misogyny and what racism is to racial bigotry and hatred (Heyward, 1989 a, b). Heterosexism is the historical social organization of our life together in which fear and uneasiness are generated toward dykes and queers–toward ourselves if we are lesbian or gay. Dialectically, these feelings serve to hold the structure in place, thereby strengthening not only such traditional patriarchal religious institutions as Christianity, which have done much to set heterosexism in place, but also more deeply personal institutions such as the self-loathing of homosexual youths and the hatred of such youths by their peers.

We might recognize heterosexism as the first born son of sexism, the structure of alienated power between men and women. Sexism refers to the historical complex of practices and attitudes essential to men's control of women's bodies and, thereby, women's lives. Heterosexism is a logical and necessary extension of sexism. It is cemented in the assumptions that male gender hegemony is good (natural, normal, moral) and that, in order to secure sexism in the social order, men must be forced, if need be, to stay in control of women's bodies.

Penetrating to the core of sexism, heterosexism heralds the recognition that, in order to keep women down, men's sexual activity must be imposed upon women. Without male control of female bodies, patriarchal power relations would not prevail: things would fall apart–for example, "romantic love" between men and women; the "ideal" of lifelong monogamous marriage and the nuclear family; "traditional values"; established religious and moral principles; the "security" and "freedom" of the nation . . . all that is predicated upon privileged men staying in control of the world as we know it.

Insofar as we recognize *heterosexism as the fundamental means of enforcing sexism,* we will realize that an analysis of gender relations cannot be separated from an analysis of sexual relations in efforts to develop adequate, trustworthy psychologies, theologies, or theories of moral reasoning.

To treat homophobia, we must understand that it is far more than a fear of homosexuality. It is the affective character of an ideological underpinning of the social order. It is an emotional undercurrent running among us generation to generation. Like men's fear of women and white people's fear of people of color, homophobia is cultivated among us via religious, educational, medical, cultural, and therapeutic traditions as a means of holding established power-relations in place–in particular, of securing male gender hegemony over women's bodies and lives.

Lesbians and gay men are homophobic too. We, like others, have been shaped within a heterosexist, homophobic social order, though I believe (with Adrienne Rich, 1978; Audre Lorde, 1984; Beverly Harrison, 1985) that homosexuality, to whatever large degree it is socially-constructed, is a form of resistance to heterosexism, whether or not lesbians and gay men individually are aware of this.

Alienation breeds many emotional problems, among them homophobia. If the Christian churches and mental health traditions were more creative, liberating institutions, we who are in them would be clear with one another, with church people, and with clients, that heterosexism is a problem facing all people–not just gay men and lesbians. We would be clear that heterosexism is our problem. Homophobia is our problem. The problem is not being gay or lesbian. We would realize that treatment, therefore, of the problem of homophobia–including its pernicious, internalized dimension among lesbians and gay men–would involve "treating" the society and its institutions, which generate homophobia and sustain heterosexism in myriad ways every day.

Consider, for example, the exclusion of benefits to gay partners by insurance policies; the rejection by the state of lesbians and gay men as foster or adoptive parents; and the countless "rituals" surrounding being born, being educated, being sexual, being married, being parents, being ill, dying and being buried. In short, we learn how to be human–how, literally, to experience our experience of ourselves–via images and innuendos of what it means to be men and women bound historically together in very particular heterosexist and homophobic ways.

There is healing to be done here for sure, and it is not of our homosexuality. Lesbians and gay men cannot be healed of our internalized homophobia, empowered to live creative, liberating lives, unless we are being called forth by therapists, religious leaders, and one another, to see that the problem is not ours as individuals. It is not a problem with origins in either our internal psychic-structures or our families of origin. The basic problem is not that we are "diseased" or that our families are or were "dysfunctional." *The problem is, basically, one of oppression and injustice.* It is a problem that belongs to the whole society. Lesbian and gay addicts cannot be healed unless we are being called forth to share a commitment to resist actively forces of heterosexism and homophobia however we can, one day at a time.

In other words, *healing must be a process of liberation with profoundly personal and political, private and public, dimensions.* In this process, the healer, whatever his or her sexuality, should not position him/herself as a "neutral" expert or observer in relation to the patient, but rather should work alongside as brother or sister, companion in the work of liberation.

ADDICTION AS A SOCIAL DIS-EASE

Like homophobia, *addiction* is a social problem, not simply an individual's disease. It seems evident that biochemical factors contribute to certain addictions, such as alcoholism (Vaillant, 1983;

Maslansky, 1989) and to certain individual's experiences of addiction. This important factor not withstanding, addiction is exacerbated by structures of alienation which form the basis of our disconnectedness from one another. Heterosexism is one such structure, as are racism, sexism, and class elitism. The major institutions of our lives under advanced patriarchal capitalism, such as dominant modes of education, religion, medicine, law, and business, are secured by these structures of alienation. As such, they contribute to our experiences of isolation from one another, each of us on his or her own, alone and separate.

The Christian religious tradition in the modern West has done much to shape a *theology of loneliness and autonomy* to undergird this alienation. The church has done so by colluding in the growth of advanced monopoly capitalism throughout the world and by fixating on the interior life of the individual as the locus of liberation–in traditional Christian language, of healing and salvation.

Two signs of the modern church's upholding of the individual as the apex of liberation are (1) the church's preoccupation with sex as virtually *the* place in which morality gets defined (i.e., morality = *sexual* morality); and (2) the liberal church's having turned to psychology–therapists, in particular–for a final word on what behavior is, or is not, "healthy," "normal," and thereby "good" in peoples' lives, especially our sex lives (Heyward, 1989 b).

In looking to psychiatry, church leaders ironically are depending on a highly individualistic medical science for help in discerning the foundational moral constitution of our collective life. This is a peculiar, but predictable dependency, since most psychiatry and traditional psychotherapeutic practices continue, like the church, to place a premium on the individual's inner growth toward becoming an autonomous, individuated self who is capable of entering into healthy, mature relationships, rather than on the *social character of our personal constitution and well-being.* (See Miller, 1988; Surrey, 1987; Jordan, 1986; Jordan, Kaplan, and Surrey, 1983; Huff, 1987; Heyward, 1989 a, b, for critique of this developmental theory.)

Because both institutions have emphasized the importance of our becoming "well-boundaried" selves, neither has reflected historically any significant appreciation of how terribly afflicted we are by the common disease of isolation. Not surprisingly, neither the Christian church nor the psychotherapeutic tradition on the whole have known how to treat alcoholics and other addicts. "Alcoholism is a disease of isolation. So, too, in their own way, are anorexia nervosa and bulimia. These are diseases of loneliness, of being cut off from the possibilities of deep, soulful, mutually empowering relationships." (Miller, 1988; Surrey, 1987, 1984).

We cannot heal diseases of isolation, loneliness, and disconnection primarily by helping people feel more autonomous, separate, and on their own. It is psychologically and ethically irresponsible for mental health professionals to stress our need for "clear boundaries" without simultaneously emphasizing our need for intimacy, solidarity, and compassion. That many therapists do not seem to comprehend why, and how, focusing on "boundaries" can be so damaging to addicts reflects the extent to which the therapeutic tradition remains, uncritically, a product of patriarchal capitalism's preoccupation with the ego of the individual (white heterosexual male) as normative in determining mental health.

Women in particular should be mindful of the nuances in this critique of autonomy. *The feminist movement is not about women becoming separate selves. It is about our discovery that our lives are connected at the root.* We are interdependent and interactive. Feminism helps us realize our lines of continuity and struggle, of love and conflict, of difference and commonality, through which we emerge as persons whose individualities are being created and sustained in the context of significant relational experiences and by strong commitments in our love and work.

This does not mean that we are, or should be, always in "a relationship." Many of us need and want solitude, singleness, and/or independence from primary relational attachments. Moreover, many of us do not want to be "coupled" but rather would choose to love in a number of primary commitments, which might or might not include explicitly sexual activity.

The relational theology, ethics, psychology, and politics implicit in these pages are meant to reflect and respond to the actual constitution of our lives. We are *not* born alone; nor do we live and die by ourselves, but rather in relation to those who have gone before, who go with us now, and who will come after us. That we do not easily feel, or honor, our interconnectedness is, I believe, the root of much pathology.

My alcoholism and eating disorder (as well as compulsive work habits) were direct consequences of my experiences of being disconnected from important relationships and from the basic constitution of the world itself. This "diseased" sensibility was no more simply my "personal" or "family" problem than homophobia is. My experience with addiction has given me an opportunity, however, to pay careful attention to the problem of addiction in order to move through it very personally as far as I can, in the company of friends, *and* in order to do something, with others, about addiction as our common problem steeped in shared experiences of radical social alienation.

To treat addiction among lesbians and gay men, we must pay critical attention to the dominant culture and its institutions that have taught us falsely that separation and autonomy should be our fundamental human aims. Two of the institutions which most effectively have promulgated these debilitating assumptions have been the Christian church and psychotherapy. Unless we are working creatively toward their transformation, we lesbian and gay addicts would do well to avoid these institutions. Normally, they will do us more harm than good. Yet, insofar as we are willing to struggle together toward their transformation, participation in church and/or therapy can provide opportunity for significant personal empowerment. This creative struggle can become itself a root of personal change and transformation.

THE 12-STEP PROGRAM

My personal journey in recovery has been simultaneously a way of participating in the struggle for justice and the beginnings of a serenity that is enabling me to relax into, and enjoy, the struggle.

For many years prior to recovery, I had been involved as both activist and theorist in justice-work in and beyond the church. Much of my work had been, I believe, good work and, most often, in the company of marvelous friends and colleagues. I had not struggled in isolation-yet, often I had *felt* alone, separate, fragmented both from others and from my most authentic, relational self.

Over time, I had begun to assume that it is impossible to be serene in the struggle. I could not imagine how we might live with a genuine sense of inner peace in the context of massive, violent resistance to justice and caring in our common life. Serenity, I assumed, was a dubious benefit of an ability to turn off a passion for justice, a yearning for mutuality and right relation in the great and small places of our lives.

And so it was that, on October 10, 1985, several days after an embarrassing public display of my "drinking problem," I mentioned to a former student, that I had decided to stop drinking the next weekend, when I'd be "alone" and, therefore, "not tempted" to drink by any social engagements. My friend's immediate response to me was stunning: "It troubles me that someone who teaches and writes so much about mutuality is so resistant to seeing that you need help with this. You can't stop drinking alone. Why don't you take your own theology seriously?"

I knew my friend was speaking the truth. That night I phoned Bonnie, the one person in New York City I knew to be in AA and asked her if she knew of a meeting (in Manhattan!) that I could attend the next day. She said she'd pick me up at 8:15 A.M.

In the morning, Bonnie and I sat together in the back row of a crowded, smoke-filled room on the Upper West Side. I said nothing, but cried, as I listened to a man, as different from me on the surface as a person could be, tell "my" story. As he spoke, I knew that he and I were connected near the core of our humanness–in our vulnerability and our need for one another's help in learning to accept and value ourselves. I told Bonnie after the meeting that I felt as if I had begun a long journey home to myself. And I had.

Before I go further, I want to say a word about the "anonymity" that is basic to the 12-Step tradition. Members of AA, OA, and other 12-Step programs interpret the anonymity tradition in different ways. To me, it is a commitment not to reveal the identities of other persons in recovery nor to exploit the 12-Step program for commercial purposes. I do not believe that the anonymity tradition should be used to inhibit either our speaking publicly about the recovery process or our sharing well-considered respectful critiques of the 12-Step program itself.

In this spirit, I shall mention here what are, in my judgment, some of the limits of the 12-Step program. Please be clear that I do not interpret these limits as reasons not to participate in the program. To suggest that something has "limits" does not mean that it is "wrong." It is much like us. To accept our limits simply means we don't expect ourselves to do what we can't do or to do more than we can do. The same should be true of our expectations of programs like AA.

SOME LIMITS OF THE PROGRAM

The 12-Step program doesn't attempt to name, analyze, or address the alienating character-structure of the larger society which generates human loneliness and isolation and which, thereby, contributes in major ways to the problem of addiction. There is no explicit, programmatic recognition that alcoholism, for example, is *not* rooted *simply* in a "diseased" individual or a "dysfunctional" family. This makes it easy for us to blame ourselves and/or our families for our being drunks, overeaters, obsessive, out of control. The blaming of ourselves, a variation on the old theme of blaming the victim, is the last thing we need to do, since it invariably is close to the heart of the problem of addiction itself. Self-blaming is related directly to experiences of isolation, loneliness, and of guilt for whatever wrong has been done, including that done to us.

Without a social analysis, the 12-Step program's spiritual dimension will remain sexist. It is difficult for many women not only to listen to sexist religious language but moreover to be met uncritically by the program's white middle-strata, male-defined, experience of what alcoholism is and what we should do about it. For instance, Alcoholics Anonymous, the "Big Book" of the program which functions like the Bible for many 12- Steppers, suggests that alcoholics can't handle anger and shouldn't be angry. This may be true for many male alcoholics (though I wonder). It most definitely does not reflect the real life-experiences of large numbers of women of all colors for whom to feel and accept our anger can be a liberating step toward health and integrity, sobriety and serenity.

Such limits of the 12-Step program should not be taken lightly. Recognizing them can be an important step in recovery for many alcoholics and addicts. There are also many alcoholics and addicts, both in recovery and not in recovery, for whom such limits as these preclude or inhibit participation in the 12-Step program. I myself have found the program sometimes troubling, often frustrating. It has also been a life-line for me, and I shall try now to tell you why.

OUR HEALING POWER IN MUTUAL RELATION

I believe the genius of the 12-Step program, which originated as Alcoholics Anonymous over 50 years ago, is its recognition of two interrelated aspects of the disease of alcoholism: (1) that alcoholism is a disease of isolation and, because this is so, (2) that recovery, or healing, is an intrinsically relational adventure with roots in a shared, ongoing discovery of mutual empowerment (Surrey, 1987; Heyward, 1989, b)–literally, the recovering of ourselves-in-relation, which is the most profound condition of our common humanity (and, some of us would add, our common experience of divinity).

In its actual practices–meetings, non-hierarchical structure, tradition of sponsorship, etc.–the program recognizes that, if our problem is one of isolation, or disconnection from right relation, our healing will be with one another, in community and connection. My friend Bonnie who accompanied me to my first meeting told me that, during her whole first year in the program, she had missed the point of AA by failing actually to hear the First Step: "*We* admitted we were powerless over alcohol, that *our* lives had become unmanageable." She had not heard the "we," but rather had held on to her misperception that she, *as an individual,* had a problem which she, *individually,* could solve. In this misperception, Bonnie had not realized the radical extent to which *we* provide the emotional, spiritual, political, and physical basis of *our* healing, together. The healing process, because it is shared, becomes genuinely a movement of liberation toward new ways of living in the world in which a passion for justice (right, mutually empowering, relation) and a sense of security (inner peace and confidence) converge.

We discover that our healing is *with* one another. The 12-Step program suggests, furthermore, that this process is enabled by the presence of a "higher" (sic) power which is called forth, or generated, in the midst of the community of recovering folks, and which empowers us. The implications of this radically embodied, relational, down-to-earth theology opens us to spirituality at its best. We are involved in godding (Heyward 1982), participants in and bearers of a spiritual power which some of us heretofore have witnessed in women's consciousness-raising groups, in the Black Church, in Nicaragua or elsewhere as Christian base communities pray together in the spirited struggle for justice.

In the 12-Step program, I am learning that healing is a radically relational adventure. I am learning that the struggle for sanity is, at root, the struggle for assurance that our lives are connected, that we are not alone. The more confident I become of our basic connectedness, and of its goodness for us, the more fully in touch with reality I am. Of this, I am confident. And what does this confidence mean for my life?

It means that I can slow down a bit. It means that I can do only what I can do, one day at a time. It means that this is good and that it is enough. There will always be others in this and other generations to carry the load with me, or for me, if I can do no more.

The confidence means that my guilt is lifted. I have less need to do it, whatever "it" may be, perfectly, or do it all, or do it now, or do it alone.

This increase in confidence, a newly-emerging serenity, means that my priorities are becoming clearer. Friendship means more to me. So too, in this spirit, does the process of mutual empowerment as the heart and soul of justice-making, in the smaller as well as the larger, public arenas of our life together.

The confidence generates joy and energy and humor. In it, I begin to see that healing really *is* part of the work of liberation;

that it's never over, never completely done; and that each day we can turn it over to the sacred spirit and let it go and that what's important will come back round to us, usually when we least expect it.

This confidence, or faith, becomes an ongoing resource of a splendid power for love and work–an empowering relational energy to struggle, in one another's company, against forces of alienation, and to celebrate, with one another, whatever is just and compassionate in the world we share as, together, we are brought more and more to our senses.

CONTRIBUTING WORKS

Fromm, E. (1961). *Marx's concept of man.* New York: Frederick Ungar.

Harrison, B.W. (1985). *Making the connections: essays in feminist social ethics.* Boston: Beacon.

Heyward, C. (1989a). "Coming out as relational empowerment: A lesbian feminist perspective." *Work in Progress*, No. 38. Wellesley, MA: Stone Center Working Paper Series.

Heyward, C. (1989b). *Touching our strength: The erotic as power and the love of God.* San Francisco: Harper and Row, Pub., Inc.

Huff, M.C. (1987). "The Interdependent self: An integrated concept from feminist theology and feminist psychology."*Philosophy and Theology*, 2 (2), 160-172.

Jordan, J.V. (1986). "The Meaning of Mutuality." *Work in Progress*, No. 23. Wellesley, MA: Stone Center Working Paper Series.

Lorde, A. (1984). "Uses of the erotic: The erotic as power." In A. Lorde, *Sister Outsider* (pp. 53-59). Trumansberg, NY: Crossing Press. (Original work published in 1978.)

Maslansky, R. (1989-90). *Psychobiology of alcoholism.* Outline of course lectures. New York, NY: New York University Medical Center. (Unpublished papers.)

Miller, J.B. (1988). "Connections, disconnections, and violations." *Work in Progress*, No. 33. Wellesley, MA: Stone Center Working Paper Series.

Rich, A. (1986). "Compulsory heterosexuality and lesbian existence." In A. Rich, *Bread, Blood, and Poetry: Selected Prose*, 1979-1985. New York: W.W. Norton & Co., Inc. (Original piece published in 1979.)

Surrey, J.L. (1984). "Eating patterns as a reflection of women's development." *Work in Progress*, No. 83-06. Wellesley, MA: Stone Center, Working Paper Series.

Surrey, J.L. (1987). "Relationship and empowerment." *Work in Progress*, No. 30. Wellesley, MA: Stone Center Working Paper Series.

Vaillant, G.E. (1983). *The natural history of alcoholism: Causes, patterns, and paths to recovery.* Cambridge: Harvard University.

Heterosexual Therapists
Treating Homosexual Addicted Clients

Vivian Ubell, ACSW
David Sumberg, ACSW

Heterosexual therapists who are treating homosexual clients suffering from an addiction need to be accepting of and comfortable with homosexuality. This acceptance must include the awareness of the therapist's own internalized homophobic feelings and thoughts as well as those of the clients. Equally important is the therapist's knowledge of addiction and the development of skills in aiding recovery.

HOMOSEXUALITY AND HOMOPHOBIA

We have all, unfortunately, been exposed to and affected by the homophobia–the irrational dread and loathing of homosexuality and homosexual people–that pervades our society (Weinberg, 1972). Equally disturbing is the fact that in our training as therapists, homophobia and heterosexism (the culturally conditioned bias that heterosexuality is intrinsically superior to homosexuality) are rarely challenged and infrequently addressed (Rochlin, 1982). There is little help for therapists who want to explore their fears, stereotypes and misconceptions about homosexuality and to alter, through knowledge and exposure, their own homophobic belief systems. Despite the fact that the American Psychiatric Association agreed in 1973 that homosexuality was not a pathological state of being, negative

Vivian Ubell and David Sumberg are both in private practice in New York City.

19

attitudes and hostile views remain prevalent in training institutions and in supervision. Open discussion of homosexual issues and frank disclosure of both positive and negative feelings about homosexuality remain the exception rather than the rule. In a three-year post-masters family therapy training program at a leading New York City family therapy institute, the issue of homosexual families and relationships was discussed fully only twice: once when a class member "came out" through sharing his genogram and once when a lesbian mother and her children were interviewed.

Homophobia that remains "underground" is particularly dangerous. Many therapists may intellectually accept homosexuality yet remain homophobic in their emotional belief systems. In a field that advocates honesty towards and acceptance of others, it is ironic to listen to the experiences of homosexual therapists who have had to remain "closeted" because of strong homophobia in their agencies or of those who have risked "coming out," only to experience subtle negative reactions from their colleagues.

In this article we would like to offer suggestions to therapists working with lesbian and gay addicted clients for coping with their countertransferential and homophobic reactions. The therapist's acceptance of homosexuality becomes crucial in helping the addicted client recover from his/her disease in which self-denial and self-hate are such significant factors.

It is detrimental to the recovery process when the therapist enters into the treatment contract with an agenda to change the client's sexual orientation, or to define it as pathological, or to explore how it evolved. The last point can be particularly damaging as the therapist's questioning can reinforce the client's own internalized homophobia and direct the beginning treatment away from recovery. Early in the treatment questions regarding sexual orientation should preferably come from the client. Subtle disapproval from the therapist, which the therapist may not be aware of, can be particularly damaging in the treatment because it is never identified as homophobic or heterosexist. It quietly undermines the client's self-acceptance.

Clients who are in recovery from addiction often suffer from low self-esteem, poor self-image, difficulty in relating, intense anxiety and deep feelings of shame. For the homosexual client there is often the additional burden of internalized homophobia resulting from the accumulated negative messages that the client has received from family, friends, society and the media. This internalized self-hatred is often unconscious or subtle and at times is expressed as confusion about sexual identity. Or, the client's, unconscious acceptance of societal homophobia may prevent them from voicing their own positive acknowledgement of their sexual orientation (Woodman and Lenna, 1982). The underlying shame appears as further confusion about sexual identity.

The therapist needs to be astute in listening for the confusion, homophobia, or heterosexism and needs to work with the client towards greater clarity and self-affirmation. Support and reassurance that the client is acceptable, valued and worthy are necessary to counteract many of the previous negative messages the client has received. When a therapist is frightened about or uncomfortable with his/her own bisexual feelings, is fearful and insecure about sexual options, or is ignorant of sexual differences, the therapy can be severely compromised. Both client and therapist may then be unable to proceed with the most important task at the beginning: the attainment of physical and emotional sobriety.

Although the first year of treatment should be strongly focused on sobriety issues (which we will discuss later), the initial contract with the client needs to address mutual comfort discussing homosexuality. At this point in the article, our focus is on cases where the homosexuality is a known factor at the beginning of treatment because the client openly presents his/her homosexuality.

There may be therapists who have never questioned their feelings about homosexual clients because they thought they did not have any homosexuals in their practice. Homosexual orientation may exist but not be acknowledged if the therapist is "closed" to knowing about it and the client is still "closeted." A parallel situation is the therapist who never asks questions about drug or alcohol use by the client and never realizes that the addiction exists. As therapists are exposed to new ideas, new life styles or new issues, they learn to ask different questions and discover new facts about their clients. For instance, when clients describe intense emotional feelings toward same sex friends or acquaintances, it is helpful for the therapist to ask whether there are also sexual feelings. Similarly, when clients describe early homosexual experiences during adolescence, therapists can inquire as to whether those feelings remain and if so, does the client allow for expression of those feelings. The therapist's own acceptance and willingness to question sets a stage for reluctant clients to reveal hidden aspects of themselves. There may also be instances when the therapist who is comfortable with homosexuality recognizes the client's latent and unstated homosexual feelings before the client has any conscious awareness of those feelings. In these instances, the therapist may help steer the client towards an exploration of those feelings when the client seems receptive.

Homosexual, addicted clients who enter treatment with an acceptance of their own sexual identity and a strong gay consciousness will rightfully question the heterosexual therapist as to his/her views and attitudes concerning homosexuality. These questions are appropriate and necessary and it is extremely important and helpful that the therapist be able to respond directly and honestly (Riess, 1987). This is a good time for therapists to question their own feelings and reactions. "Am I feeling defensive about my views on homosexuality?" "Is the desire to ask why the client is asking, masking my own confusion about the topic?" "Am I fearful of my reactions to hearing the details of my client's life?" It is important to emphasize that this self-questioning is crucial to the therapists' awareness of their acceptance of homosexuality as it is with other difficult and controversial issues.

In a recent first session, Paul asked, "Are you gay?" The therapist responded, "No." Paul then asked, "How can you then know what I'm going through? What it's like for me to be gay? How can you help me?" The therapist said, "That's true. I can't know what it's like for you to be gay." The therapist further explained that what is most important is hearing from Paul what being gay is like for him, what his experiences have been and how he feels about those experiences. The therapist also added that it was quite essential for the therapist to get feedback from him if he ever felt the therapist did not understand either him or the social context in which he experienced his life.

The therapist appreciated Paul's questions and did not experience them as an attempt to dismiss or discount the therapist's skill. Although the therapist had a lot of knowledge of the lesbian and gay community and many homosexual clients, the therapist didn't know if any of their experiences necessarily matched Paul's experiences. The session continued smoothly and the focus shifted to Paul's work on his sobriety (he had been sober for three weeks).

At no point should the therapist try to deny that societal responses to heterosexual life and homosexual life are different. The heterosexual therapist does not experience homosexual life except as analogy, and the acknowledgment of this truth often strengthens the bond between client and therapist.

In some instances in working with addicted clients (no matter what the sexual preference), questions regarding "difference" between the client and the therapist, can become attempts to distance oneself from sobriety and can become the excuse to use the addictive substance again. If a recovering client feels misunderstood by the therapist at a time when sobriety seems weak and may be at stake, the therapist may want to interpret the client's labeling everyone as different and therefore unable to understand the client's life as the desire to again become isolated and ultimately to return to using drugs again.

In other instances, the client may just need to report direct differences or examples of homophobic experiences which need to be explored and acknowledged.

Being gay affirming, or being determined "not to reinforce in gay and lesbian clients the devaluing messages issuing from the culture," and offering clients the view that being lesbian or gay is a positive identity (Hall, 1985) are essential for the heterosexual therapist working with the gay client.

With homosexual addicted clients who are themselves homophobic and have little gay consciousness, the therapist's ability to be gay affirming is even more critical because of clients' great need of formulating and accepting a positive sense of sexual identity once sober.

CONSCIOUSNESS RAISING FOR THERAPISTS

To gain more knowledge about and a sense of ease with homosexuality as a heterosexual therapist, we make a number of suggestions.

First, pay close attention to one's own attitudes, premises and feelings about homosexuality. "The homophobia in ourselves, as well as in others is always dangerous, but it is particularly lethal when it goes underground" (Hall, 1985). The homophobia, whether in the client or the therapist, needs to be an open subject in the therapy and in the therapist's life. It is also helpful if therapists can acknowledge and accept the homosexual potential in themselves (Markowitz, 1991). Awareness and acceptance are forerunners to change for ourselves and for our clients. Be alert for subtle disapproval. Acknowledgment of the differences between therapists and clients can be helpful and provide validation of clients' experience in their families, where misunderstandings of the difference between homosexuality and heterosexuality often occurred (Markowitz, 1991). The therapist's candor can help clients and their families (when family sessions are held) move from denial of their homophobia to recognition of the pervasive prejudice that devalues lesbians and gays in this society (Dahlheimer and Feigal, 1991).

In one session, Ruth, a mother of 7-year-old Amy, whom she co-parented with her lover Pam, talked about their fear of going to open school night and presenting themselves to the teacher as Amy's mothers. At first the therapist supported her fears and thinking that the teacher might not accept their lesbianism and life style and possibly treat Amy as "different." The therapist thought about it further and realized it was a homophobic reaction that supported Ruth's homophobia. She was not feeling comfortable and accepting of her life style choices. It would also be very detrimental to Amy to have to hide her actual life situation from her teacher and her classmates. There was nothing to be ashamed of and if the teacher had a negative reaction, perhaps Ruth and Pam could educate their child, and if necessary, explain the teacher's homophobia to their child.

At this point, the therapist said to Ruth, "As you were talking, I initially felt support for your views but I think we both might be reacting homophobically," and asked if there had been any prior experiences with the teacher that led to her present fears. Ruth said, "No." She was very relieved to hear the therapist's views and thoughts and realized how burdensome her own internalized homophobia had become in this situation. Ultimately, the mothers were able to go to parents' night with a positive affirmation of their life style and of their relationship. The teacher was accepting and already knew of the home situation from Amy.

Secondly, if you have homosexual friends, spend time with them and share their lives, ask questions and learn from their experiences.

Thirdly, read from varied sources. Autobiographies and novels in which homosexual relationships are described can provide insights into homosexuality. Contact lesbian and gay organizations for suggestions of readings and other materials. Current therapeutic readings that provide consciousness raising for the therapist can be helpful. *Family Therapy Networker* (January/February 1991) recently devoted an issue to therapy dealing with lesbian and gay relationships and provided excellent case material, suggestions and questions for therapists. Some of its suggestions include seeking out a co-therapy experience or supervision with a lesbian or gay therapist, seeing the all too few movies and TV shows that deal with homosexuality, or joining in events that support lesbian and gay rights (Dahlheimer and Feigal, 1991).

Finally, if as the therapist you experience feelings of disgust, repulsion, disapproval or anger at the client's choice of a homosexual life style, consider removing yourself from the case, without blaming the client (supervision can help in this process). Not every therapist has to be able to help every client.

DEALING WITH ADDICTION

Knowledge of addiction and its treatment is the other crucial factor in dealing with homosexual, addicted clients. Maintaining a consistent and primary focus on physical and emotional sobriety is a critical factor in the addict's recovery regardless of whether the addict is heterosexual or homosexual. Marny Hall (1985) writes,

> Gay affirmation is an indispensable part of effective therapy with lesbians and gay men. Good therapy, however, is not limited to lesbian and gay issues. Plenty of problems, although they may be indirectly related to sexual orientation,

have a reality independent of lesbianism or gayness. Such problems, which must be dealt with separately, include: drug or alcohol abuse . . . (p.97).

Physical sobriety refers to the absence of the addictive substance from the client's life. Emotional sobriety encompasses the attitudinal changes that need to accompany physical sobriety and are often learned in the 12-Step self-help programs. Familiarity with the 12-Step programs, a good understanding of the actual 12 steps, how meetings are run, where and when local meetings are scheduled and how the program operates can facilitate the client's involvement. This knowledge can be acquired by reading the literature, by listening to and asking questions of clients in the programs, and by attending "open" meetings oneself in order to learn through experience. Heterosexual and homosexual therapists who themselves are in recovery can directly share their experiences with their clients. At times, we have found it helpful to offer to accompany a reluctant client to a meeting. The power of the therapist's willingness to take time to attend a meeting often reinforces the importance of the program for the client, helps the client overcome fears and resistance, and strengthens the therapeutic alliance.

Further, knowledge of lesbian and gay services in the community and 12-Step meetings that may be specifically listed as homosexual is helpful. Unfortunately, these resources are extremely limited in some parts of the country. Lesbian clients who have or desire a feminist orientation can familiarize themselves with a feminist conceptualization of the 12-Step programs (Kosl, 1990).

If homosexual clients feel uncomfortable at heterosexual meetings, and there are no homosexual groups available, it is sometimes helpful to point out that it is the "program," not the personalities, that is important. Often, the similarities in how the addiction has affected lives are more important for recovery than the differences between homosexual and heterosexual life styles. Emphasizing similarities while acknowledging differences helps the client to accept the real help found in the 12-Step programs.

However, when homophobia is encountered by the client at a straight AA meeting, or the client reports back to the therapist that no one at the meeting shares his/her experiences with life, exploration and acknowledgement are needed. For some clients, straight meetings are not supportive enough and clients are not able to be honest about their sexual orientation because of overt anti-homosexual statements in the rooms. This takes a heavy toll on clients who can not be honest in a program that promotes honesty. Once again, clients feel a need to hide their sexuality. Some lesbian and gay clients who live in areas where there is no supportive network for their homosexuality attend AA regional lesbian and gay round-up meetings (weekend-long marathon meetings) which are places that homosexuals in recovery can meet each other. For others, supportive readings can be helpful.

In the first year of recovery from an addiction, it is particularly critical to make sobriety the primary focus. "Other issues" can often be presented by the client as an attempt to create a defensive smokescreen arising from the "addicted self" and to sidetrack the work on sobriety. Sometimes, even in later years of recovery, this occurs. The therapist working with the addicted, homosexual client can help the client understand that if the client does not maintain sobriety as a primary focus, then any other desired therapeutic work on lesbian or gay issues will be destroyed by the disease becoming active.

In one case, Ellen and Carol entered treatment complaining of tension, conflicts and arguments about the lack of sex in the relationship. As the situation was explored and a history regarding addiction was taken (it is extremely important to ask questions of *all* clients in one's practice about substance abuse and use, including any family history of substance abuse), it became apparent that the problems primarily concerned issues of sobriety. Ellen had a long history of alcohol and cocaine abuse but had been chemically free from these for the past four years. However, although she had maintained her physical sobriety, she had ceased attending any 12-Step meetings for the past two years. This coincided with her entering into the relationship with Carol. She had become angry shortly after the couple had begun living together two years ago. She was living an emotionally "unsober" life, with frequent, explosive outbursts and strong moodiness which led to feelings of shame and remorse. This behavior was reminiscent of her behavior when she had been a substance abuser and she spoke about feeling "high" during these fights.

Carol was now in her third relationship with an active or recovering substance abuser. As a child, she had been the caretaker of her depressed and alcoholic mother. In her relationship with Ellen, Carol always tried to correct Ellen's moods or "make things better" so that Ellen wouldn't explode. She always felt responsible for Ellen's outbursts and would apologize for everything. However, she internally felt resentful and abused by the relationship and acted out her own anger by withholding sex. This description is typical of the classic "co-dependent" in the addictive relationship.

The therapist told the couple that she would be glad to address the sexual issues in the relationship at a later date but that the couple needed to address the addictive issues in the relationship first.

Ellen quickly recognized that she had returned to an addictive pattern of behavior and that she wasn't "emotionally sober." She began attending 12-Step meetings regularly and found that her anger subsided and she had better ways of expressing it.

Carol needed education and support from the therapist before she was willing to attend co-dependent and Alanon 12-Step meetings. After several meetings, however, she began to talk more about her childhood and how her own needs hadn't been met. With time she was able to take less responsibility for Ellen's behavior and to focus more on her own needs and anger. The sexual problems needed only minimal attention after the couple developed a more "sober" relationship.

In another example of using issues to avoid sobriety, Sam argued intensively with the therapist that gay men had no other choice but to go to gay bars. Sam said that he often found it harder to maintain his sobriety when going to bars but added, "How am I to meet anyone?" He insisted that he wanted to be sober but that the bar scene often broke down his resolve. When the therapist suggested that perhaps he was ambivalent about really embracing his sobriety, he responded that the therapist just didn't understand the "gay life style." The therapist did not accept this redefinition of the problem, knowing that there were many gay sober activities in the community, and gently suggested to Sam that there were alternative ways to socialize. Concrete suggestions were then provided. The therapist listened empathetically to Sam's difficulty in breaking away from the bar scene, but repeatedly brought the discussion back to Sam's underlying reluctance to really address his drinking problem. Sam agreed finally to begin attending gay AA meetings which provided him with a place to really work on his sobriety as well as a sober, supportive, social gay network.

In areas of the country where there are no sober supportive activities for homosexuals, the bar may be the only place to go for contact with other homosexuals. The recovering client then needs to learn how to go to the bar but not partake in the alcoholic activity.

DEALING WITH SEXUAL IDENTITY AND SOBRIETY

As the addictive cloud lifts, the client begins to be more conscious of feelings. Shame, fear, anxiety, pain, hurt, confusion, guilt, remorse often emerge as the sober client allows the feelings to be conscious. Exhilaration, hope, joy, love and excitement are also present as the client begins to feel grounded in the recovery. Often, the addictive behavior was an attempt to deny deep feelings of shame, confusion and fear of the homosexual identity. After learning how to be without the addictive substance on a physical level, recovering addicts can learn who they are and begin to accept honestly both the positive and negative parts of themselves. Letting go of the shame about themselves both as addicts and as gay people is essential. The "owning" of oneself is an important aspect of the 12-Step programs and when lesbian or gay 12-Step programs are available, the combined aspects of the programs are powerful in healing.

Because addiction also can hide "true self" feelings, after sobriety is achieved a heterosexual client may discover strong homosexual feelings. In these instances, the therapist's acceptance of these homosexual feelings is essential for the maintenance of the sobriety and the emerging self. As the client explores the emerging feelings and fears, the therapist needs to maintain a reassuring, empathic and accepting posture. For some clients there has been a dilemma as to how to stay sober and face their sexuality. One client said "I always knew I drank so I wouldn't have to face this part of myself." The therapist responded, "I feel it's very sad that you have had to avoid and hide positive aspects of yourself." The client needed to trust the therapist's ability to accept their homosexual feelings.

FAMILY OF ORIGIN ISSUES

During recovery, family of origin issues also arise. In addition to understanding the role of addiction in the extended family, the therapist needs to explore with the client the family's acceptance of homosexuality. The 12-Step concept that people are only as "sick" as their secrets, sometimes applies in this case. When the homosexuality is kept secret from the family because of shame, the "coming out" process may be very powerful and healing and may further the recovery.

Lending emotional and concrete support to the client during the "coming out" process can be valuable for the therapeutic process. Coaching clients in role plays and discussions that prepare for the "coming out" can be helpful at times. In some instances, the therapist can have clients write a letter to their parents or other family members that expresses their feelings about their sexual preferences, relationships, resentments, hopes, desires, etc. The therapist can then rework the letter with the client as needed to help engage the family in a new dialogue and relationship.

Sometimes, bringing in the extended family is appropriate. Often clients may choose to "come out" to the family in the therapy room with the therapist's support. The therapist's ability to join with the family while maintaining a primary alliance with the client can facilitate the family's acceptance. The therapist's non-judgmental and accepting posture may provide important modeling for the family.

If the client has been cut off by the family, then the therapist, as a "representation" of an accepting family member, may be critical. If the family has rejected the client, it is once again important to feel comfortable with the client's anger in the transference. The therapist needs to accept the validity of the anger and be prepared to discuss the individual, familial and societal heterosexism and its impact on the client.

In the following case, the therapist's support for the client's homosexual identity was particularly significant to the client's recovery. John, age 30, entered treatment shortly after having completed a one-month rehabilitation program for his heavy use of alcohol and occasional use of cocaine. He grew up in a family of six children with an abusive and alcoholic father. It is not uncommon for addicted clients to have grown up in addicted households, and we again stress that a careful family history regarding addiction should be taken. His father, from the time he was eight, humiliated John for his "feminine" traits (crying easily, not liking rough sports, etc). From an early age, John remembers feeling sexually interested in other boys and feeling shamed by his father's label of "faggot." Feelings of shame were intensified when his siblings came to call him "faggot" as well.

Throughout his adolescence and adulthood he kept his homosexuality secret from friends, family, and in many ways, from himself. He frequented the back rooms of gay bars and avoided any public acknowledgment of gay identity.

With sobriety, John began to talk about his shame and difficulty in ever feeling pride in his sexual orientation. The therapist's open support of homosexuality was something John had never experienced from anyone and he slowly began to accept it. After two years of the therapist's suggestions that he might enjoy contact with gay organizations (John was attending AA meetings during this time and avoiding any meetings listed as homosexual), John finally went to a gay ACOA meeting (Adult Children of Alcoholics). This meeting had a profound effect on John's life and on his treatment. He felt enormous relief in no longer feeling "alone" with his problems, and the issues that other ACOA members raised triggered many important memories for John. Over the next year, he came out to his family (his father was no longer alive), became a leader in a number of gay organizations, and became involved in a long term, satisfying, gay relationship. John later revealed in therapy that the therapist's heterosexuality had made the support of his homosexuality that much more powerful. He wasn't sure, because of his own internalized homophobia, whether he would have been able to give as much validity or weight to suggestions if the therapist had been homosexual as well. He was sad to admit that aspect of his earlier "demeaning" self, but was also proud that in his new consciousness he could feel whole and sober in his life and take great pride in his gayness.

DEALING WITH SOCIETY, SEXUAL IDENTITY AND SOBRIETY

Because of societal homophobia and heterosexist views, the therapist does need to be cognizant of the reality of the client's being subjected frequently to the society's homophobia. Although the client can hopefully achieve an open, positive, sober and self-affirming sexual identity in the therapy room, in some instances it may be unwise for the client to be "out of the closet."

Judges still deny custody to lesbian mothers in some parts of the country (Dahlheimer and Feigal, 1991). People still lose jobs, receive subtle and not-so-subtle harassment, and fear reprisals. In these instances, it is important for the client to be encouraged to develop sober support systems, where available, in the lesbian and gay community that create a nurturing environment for self-acceptance and a positive sense of sexual identity in order to deal with the conflicts. In addition, anger towards the therapists's heterosexuality, as a representation of the injustices that the client has experienced, may be expressed. The therapist needs to tolerate and understand the anger and empathize with the client's feelings. The fact that the therapist accepts the anger as valid and as a reaction to actual prejudice helps clients feel less alone in their struggles with the outside world.

The heterosexual therapist also needs to be sensitive to the differences between rural environments and urban environments. Sober lesbian and gay resources are much more limited in rural environments. The gay affirming stance of the therapist may be particularly significant for the client who has minimal opportunities for contact with other homosexual people.

Finally, sexual mores, customs and traditions are always changing in the homosexual community just as they do in the heterosexual community. There are many homosexual "life styles." Often, with recovery, as a more true and sober self emerges, clients may look to make changes. A client, Arthur, had always been a wonderful caretaker of his lovers when he had been a drinker. He fed them, cleaned the house, ironed, paid for vacations, and was always angry at the lack of reciprocity. When sober, he realized he had taken on many stereotypical roles and looked to change his relationships into ones with more equality.

It is helpful for the therapist to be familiar with issues such as monogamy, power and control, distance and closeness, as they manifest themselves in lesbian and gay relationships. Staying abreast of the changes and not getting rooted in stereotypes and old belief systems is important. Each lesbian and gay addicted client has a different life story, and it is crucial for the therapist to accept the individual differences, help the client discover his/her own path for recovery and place the individual's experience into a larger, sober and societal framework.

REFERENCES

Dahlheimer, D. and Feigal, J. (1991, January/February). Bridging the gap. *Family Therapy Networker*, 44-53.

Hall, M. (1985). *The lavender couch: A consumer's guide to psychotherapy for lesbians and gay men*. Boston: Alyson Publications, Inc. 92-105.

Kosl, C.D. (1990, November/December). The twelve step controversy. *Ms. Magazine*, 30-31.

Markowitz, L. (1991, January/February). Homosexuality: Are we still in the dark? *Family Therapy Networker* 27-35.

Riess, B. (1987). Transference and countertransference in therapy with homosexuals. *Dynamic Psychotherapy*, 5, (2), 117-129.

Rochlin, M. (1982). Sexual orientation of the therapist and therapeutic effectiveness with gay clients. In J. Gonsiorek (Ed.), Homosexuality and psychotherapy; A practitioner's handbook of affirmative models. *Journal of Homosexuality* 7, (2/3), New York: The Haworth Press, Inc. 21-29.

Weinberg, G. (1972). *Society and the healthy homosexual*. New York, St. Martins.

Woodman, N.J. and Lenna, H.R. (1982). *Counseling with gay men and women; A guide for facilitating positive life styles*, San Francisco: Jossey-Bass Inc., Publishers, 44-47.

Substance Abuse and AIDS: Report from the Front Lines (The Impact on Professionals)

Michael Shernoff, MSW, ACSW
Edith Springer, MSW, ACSW

Working with chemically dependent people and working with people with HIV Spectrum Disease both present great challenges to the health care practitioner. Aside from the major professional challenges of locating scarce resources and quality medical care, drug treatment or psychosocial services, there are issues of stigma, discrimination and fears which add more difficulty and stress to the social worker or counselor's job. The nature of HIV Spectrum Disease and chemical dependency bring up many emotional reactions in the worker which can interfere with optimal delivery of services to clients. These reactions, which are called countertransference, must be acknowledged and resolved as much as possible in order to prevent their impacting negatively on the services being delivered and their reception by the client.

The importance of being aware of one's reactions is particularly crucial when working with individuals who are both gay or lesbian and chemically dependent, for these clients have multiple risks and often complex issues to resolve. Gay men may have risk from sexual behavior and present or former drug use behaviors. Gay men in recovery, who may have given up risky drug related behaviors years ago, can find a new pull toward drug use due to their

Michael Shernoff is Co-Director of Chelsea Psychotherapy Associates.

Edith Springer is Supervising Program Development Specialist at the New Jersey AIDS Education Center at the University of Medicine and Dentistry of New Jersey.

anxieties about HIV. For those who have not been HIV tested and do not know their status, there may be fears about both past sexual and past drug related activities. And, if gay men in recovery had a history of working in the sex industry, there is even higher risk. For those who have tested HIV negative, there are still fears about the future and there may also be survivor's guilt for people who participated in high risk behaviors and didn't get HIV. Gay men and lesbians in general have suffered many losses since the HIV pandemic began and grief overload can be a pull toward drugs as a coping mechanism. Lesbians who have been drug injectors have often had to resort to selling sex to men in order to survive in the illegal and expensive world of drugs. Their risk then, is threefold: sex with women, sex with men and sharing injection equipment. Often, HIV education has not focused on behaviors and many lesbians have been unaware of their risk, thinking that their "group" cannot get HIV infection. It is important to add that since any use of mood altering substances (even legal ones, like alcohol) prior to sex often results in unsafe sex, gay men and lesbians do not have to be addicted or chemically dependent to have risk associated with their recreational drug use.

The authors have worked in both fields–AIDS and substance abuse–and have drawn many parallels between these fields. Workers in both areas of practice often complain of feeling overwhelmed and burdened by countertransference which, if not dealt with in an adaptive fashion, can lead to burnout. In an effort to guide practitioners through the process of identifying countertransference and coping adaptively, the authors will present some of their own experiences and some of the ways they were able to work through their feelings so that the goal of assisting the client to achieve a better quality of life could be achieved.

"Countertransference reactions refer to the health care provider's conscious or unconscious behavioral, cognitive, or emotional reactions to the circumstances, emotions, or behaviors presented by the client" (Macks, 1988). Objective countertransference refers to feelings induced by the client that would be induced in any worker as, for example, when a client behaves in a hostile manner and threatens a worker verbally. Any worker would be afraid of an aggressive threat. Subjective countertransference refers to feelings which come from the worker's history or unconscious which are not universal feelings the client would induce in any worker but are particular to that worker, for example, the worker is homophobic and has difficulty working with gay clients. In general, objective countertransference is grist for the therapeutic mill–that is, it can be used to reflect back to the client how his or her behavior produces reactions in others and can be helpful in developing the client's observing ego. Subjective countertransference, on the other hand, must be recognized by the worker and resolved so that it does not impact negatively upon the client (Luban and Salon, 1981-84).

Substance abuse treatment is often seen as a hopeless task. Drug treatment modalities are not successful with many of the clients they serve. The drug-free therapeutic communities struggle with the issue of retention in treatment, as many of their entrants leave before treatment is completed; the methadone maintenance system fares better with retention, but finds a large percentage of its clients abusing drugs while in treatment (Sorrell, 1990). Detoxification, largely misunderstood as a treatment modality when it is at best a medical intervention required in many cases before treatment can begin, has been proven to be extremely unsuccessful with addicts (NIDA, 1981). The Pilot Needle Exchange Study in New York City reports that of one group of 56 of its program participants who were referred to and entered drug treatment (methadone maintenance or drug free program) 34 (64%) remained in treatment longer than 60 days and 20 (36%) remained less than 60 days. Thirty-eight of the group had previous drug treatment experience which had obviously not been successful (NYC Department of Health, 1989).

How do workers in the field cope with the low success rates in the treatment of substance abuse? One of the ways, particularly for those in methadone maintenance, is to redefine success. Successful drug treatment is often seen as abstinence. In fact, our abstinence bias has created a stigmatization of methadone maintenance as a modality. Workers hear their colleagues asking, "How can you work in methadone; all you're doing is substituting one drug for another." Although there are many models for chemotherapy relative to other diseases (e.g., insulin treatment for diabetes) those who do not acknowledge chemical dependency as a disease are unable to see methadone as a viable treatment which allows clients to leave the street world of crime and the unhealthy lifestyle produced by the illegality of drugs and their high cost. Likewise, in AIDS work, many people cannot see how workers can take on a job that will end in the premature death of the client despite improved medical treatments. If a worker is "cure" oriented in either the substance abuse field or the AIDS field, hopelessness, helplessness and burnout will certainly follow. By redefining success, not as curing the client of the disease, but as enhancing and improving the clients' quality of life for whatever time they have left, workers can eliminate the hopeless feeling and feel good about their work. A methadone client who is no longer being arrested and incarcerated for crimes undertaken to get money for drugs, whose family is rejoined, who is able to obtain permanent housing and a more stable income, can be seen as a success in treatment. The fact he or she may remain on methadone is inconsequential. A person with AIDS who is able to continue working for several years after diagnosis, take vacations, complete important life tasks and enjoy friends and family, who can continue to contribute to the community until shortly before death by adopting a "Living with AIDS" model rather than allowing needless debilitation marks a success in treatment. By redefining the markers of success both workers and clients can feel that their work together is helpful and positive.

Working with people in crisis can produce feelings of frustration and a sense of running around in circles and never getting to the long term goals set by the worker and the client. Clients in drug treatment and People With AIDS often move rapidly from one crisis to another. People involved with HIV are often on emotional roller coasters due to mental and physical status that can fluctuate from day to day and even hour to hour. Drug treatment clients coming to the program intoxicated may also produce negative feelings in the worker. The worker needs to be prepared to accompany the client through each new medical, interpersonal, intrapsychic or practical emergency that may emerge, without getting on the emotional roller coaster with the client. Constant crisis states give the work a rushed quality and make the worker feel like he/she is applying band-aids rather than getting to the core of the client's problem. Many of the crises involve concrete issues and entitlements, which some workers feel are less important than counseling or therapy and prefer not to deal with them. Perhaps one way to avoid burnout is to see crisis work as very important to the client and the re-stabilization of his or her life as a primary goal that must be reached before any other work can begin. From the client's perspective, case management and the provision of concrete services and entitlements may be the most important roles practitioners can assume.

The worker must be flexible and professionally creative while still remaining "appropriate." It is difficult to maintain one's boundaries, particularly during times when the client is regressed due to crisis and an inability to cope. The profound human suffering and tragedy experienced by those with HIV spectrum disease and those involved with drugs often provokes a strong emotional response on the part of the worker. Most of us enter the "helping professions" because of our compassion and desire to help others; the work constantly tugs on the strings of our hearts. Many of us have a giant rescue fantasy and parental feelings towards clients. We feel we are going to make the client's life better. We need to look at this grandiosity and see it as disempowering to the client. Only the client can make his or her life better; we can facilitate the process, but only if we are aware of our limitations. AIDS and chemical dependency are two diseases which humble us as workers.

Sometimes AIDS teaches us to throw the book away. Admonitions not to ever touch a client are often simply not relevant. In a situation in which a 30 year old black woman diagnosed with AIDS Related Complex had spent three months in a hospital without ever being touched by human hands (without latex gloves), the patient was experiencing stimulus hunger and craved the feeling of a caring hand. The social worker found her crying in her bed one day, and the client said she realized that "no one is ever going to touch me again as long as I live." The client felt toxic and untouchable. Initially the worker heard her supervisor's "tapes" playing in her head, "Never touch a client." With her guilt mounting, the worker reached out to take the client in her arms. The worker learned that the new disease AIDS brings new rules. Now, it is important for workers to touch clients to counteract stimulus hunger, belie the feeling of toxicity and provide caring interventions in a way that will help the client. Similarly, crying with a client has been considered "inappropriate" for a worker in traditional settings. Sometimes a genuine empathic response to the client's situation needs to be expressed for both the worker and the client. How much grief can a worker absorb and sit on?

There are many old admonitions which need to be re-examined. For example, one of the reasons given for not touching clients is that it might eroticize the transference. In the case above discussed, the worker was a heterosexual female and the client was a lesbian. Hugging and touching the client did in fact eroticize the transference. The following day the client gave a seductive smile to the worker and said, "Let's go to a hotel and fool around." The worker felt she had made a mistake and felt guilty, but went on to process the issue with the client. They discussed the role of the worker in the client's life and the fact that the worker, whether sexually attracted to the client or not, could not ignore the professional boundaries inherent in the client-worker relationship. The client understood the boundary and knew that no romance or sex could occur between them: however, she asked the worker if the worker minded a little flirting because no one else was visiting her and there was no opportunity for her to feel like a sexual being. The worker was amenable to the flirting, which then continued for a few days and eventually stopped. No harm was done and, in fact, once the issue was out in the open, both client and worker felt more comfortable.

Substance abuse workers are instructed never to work with a client while he or she is under the influence of mood altering substances. We stop counseling sessions, whether group or individual, to reflect to the client that he/she is high and needs to reschedule the session for a time when the client will be sober. Active drug and alcohol users with HIV infection and/or illness desperately need counseling, support, case management and assistance in countless areas of their lives. Therefore, workers must reevaluate the conventional wisdom of not working with a client who is high. Committed long term drug users will receive no HIV related services if that position is taken during the AIDS epidemic. Of the 260,000 drug addicts in New York State, only about 50,000 or approximately one-fifth can enter treatment due to the lack of treatment slots (N.Y.S.D.S.A.S., 1989). The other 210,000 who are at high risk for HIV deserve the same assistance as those who are in treatment. Drug users may never make the decision to give up drugs; certainly the point of an ARC or AIDS diagnosis is not a good time to try to force abstinence on a long time user with few other coping mechanisms. The first rule of social work, "Start where the client is at" demands that we offer help to the intoxicated client. Workers must look at their own issues about drug use and their understanding of the problem: chemical dependency is a disease, not a moral issue. Discrimination based on what disease a person has is unacceptable, as is homophobic or racist discrimination.

Many people view dying and death in a highly romanticized way. They have the idea that as people die they become transformed into spiritual beings. For some people this is the case, but most people die in character. Not every dying person is nice or even likeable. Working with dying people who are angry, hostile, demanding or manipulative can be particularly difficult for the worker who may already be stressed by the fact that the client is dying. The reality is that dying does not usually transform people into accepting, serene people who have resolved their issues and are gracefully closing their lives; the worker must accept the client as he or she is and put the fantasies from the movies aside.

One of the most difficult pieces of countertransference workers suffer from is over-identification with the client. While this can occur in any setting, it is particularly devastating in AIDS and in substance abuse when the client is the same age or younger, maybe is in the same ethnic group as the worker or has the same sexual orientation as the worker. Perhaps the worker has abused drugs in the past or is in recovery now. Workers in both fields may have the same high risk factors for HIV infection as the clients. One of the writers is a gay man who is infected with HIV. The other writer is a former heroin addict who had been involved in prostitution. One aspect of this work that is particularly stressful is that it causes the worker to face issues in his or her own life and behaviors, past history and mortality. Many gay men and many recovering drug users find they are not able to deal with issues around

HIV in their practice because they have been unable to resolve their own issues and fears. Others may push ahead to confront these issues in their practices in the unconscious hope that it will keep AIDS away from them. Clinical supervision is essential to help workers identify their own boundary weaknesses and magical thinking and take steps to counteract them.

In our death-denying culture each of us carries around an illusion of our own immortality. Working with clients who are in the final stages of their lives shatters this illusion and forces us to confront the reality of our own vulnerability. If left unexamined by the - worker this can result in emotional distancing from the client. This distancing will negatively affect the client's ability to discuss subjects about which they can talk to no one else. By allowing the client to discuss death and dying and issues of mortality, the worker will eventually become less afraid and can be helpful to the client and to him/herself in becoming more comfortable with death.

Physical and mental deterioration in a young client brings up many feelings. The AIDS dementia complex that many HIV clients manifest often brings a premature geriatric-type state that may have a rapid and sudden onset or appear in a gradual progression. Helping clients manage memory loss, confusion and violent mood swings while they adjust to the physical deterioration and disfigurement of their illness takes a toll on both client and worker. Many times the worker dreads seeing the once-healthy client in an emaciated, weak and unattractive state. For those unfamiliar with work in medical settings, walking into a hospital room to see one's client hooked up to machines and tubes, smelling bad and looking extremely ill can be a traumatic experience. Many workers avoid visiting their clients in hospital for this reason. Yet the continuity of care that a worker provides in making such visits is crucial to the client's quality of life. Workers need to desensitize themselves by placing themselves in hospitals and among People With AIDS so they can become inured to the sights, sounds, and smells of illness.

A particularly difficult period for the therapist occurs when exploring with a terminally ill client his/her feelings about wanting to terminate medical treatment or end his/her own life. The complex emotional, ethical and legal questions this raises for the worker can be particularly taxing when the client is sane and discussing suicide rationally. How one deals with suicidal ideations and plans as a worker has always been extremely clear: one does everything in one's power to prevent suicide. Before AIDS, we always did. Now the certainty of how to handle a suicidal client has become somewhat blurred. A terminally ill client who feels he/she has no quality of life and who is in severe pain and emotional anguish, who may be unable to relate to those who love him/her and whom they love, who may be demented or showing signs of neuropsychiatric deterioration, or who may be blind or unable to move and who considers suicide is often making a rational choice. They need to discuss that option with their worker without being rushed to the Psychiatric Emergency Room or put on psychotropic medication or in some way prevented from making their decision and acting on it. In the experience of the writers, very few clients attempt suicide, but almost all of the PWAs we've worked with have needed to hold it as an option and think of it when they felt they could not go on. It is very difficult for a well trained health care professional to sit and rationally discuss suicide with a client and not run for a psychiatric consult. Often when clients discuss suicide they are feeling particularly unloved or burdensome to those they love and need reassurance from care partners and family that they are still loved and valued as people.

A client in a residential drug treatment facility in upstate New York was diagnosed with AIDS. He told his counselor he was going to leave treatment and go home to spend the remainder of his life fishing and relaxing with his family. The worker knew that the client would go back to drugs since treatment had only just begun and the client's sobriety was shaky. The worker still agreed with the client, saying, "That's what I would do if I had AIDS." The worker was giving up on the client and later admitted to being relieved at not having to work with the client and watch him suffer and die. The worker colluded with the client's denial and actually supported the client in giving up. The client left treatment and returned to drug use, shortening his life and destroying the quality of whatever time he had left. In working with clients, what *we* would do is not to be pushed upon the client. We have a professional role to fulfill with the client and we need to keep our objectivity. One way of preventing the intrusion of the worker's choices into the client's treatment is to conduct all counseling with the goal of fulfilling the needs of the *client*. There are no absolutes in terms of right and wrong in dealing with the human condition; and the worker's values, beliefs and goals are secondary in importance to those of the client. When a client states a decision, the worker's job is to explore that decision with the client to insure that the client feels that it is the best choice under the circumstances; if both client and worker agree that it is, the worker should help the client achieve the aims the client has established. If the worker has reservations about the client's decision, those reservations should be presented; the client's decision must still be respected and supported.

Abandonment is an issue for workers when clients disappear or die. Often there is no opportunity to formally terminate with clients, either because a sudden decision is made to relocate the client elsewhere, e.g., to their family in another state or to a hospital or nursing home, or the client disappears from outpatient treatment with no notice of where he/she is going or dies suddenly and unexpectedly. The stress of being left and not knowing what has happened and the stress of incomplete work can lead to a feeling of incompetence on the part of the worker. This is not a new phenomenon to drug treatment workers. Clients may suddenly disappear due to overdose, violent death, incarceration or running from the authorities or criminal underworld. Not infrequently the worker never finds out what happened and thinks about the client on and off for years, wondering. Sometimes the worker later finds out what happened to the client. Workers whose client contact is abruptly aborted need good clinical supervision to deal with the inability to know or to finish up with these clients. Workers need the termination phase of treatment as much as clients do. Both suffer when termination does not occur.

When a client dies, regardless of the setting or the reason, workers need to have structures and methods for grieving. Sometimes a "post-mortem" case conference can help workers look at the case and put some closure on it. Sometimes agencies ignore the need for workers to grieve and in fact regard grieving workers as inappropriate. Where workers can openly mourn their clients, burnout is reduced and other clients see the real care and concern that workers have for them. Attending wakes, funerals and memorial services for clients is very important for workers who wish to do so. Many drug treatment programs have a practice of posting a photograph of a deceased client with a small statement about the person where everyone can see it, allowing both staff and clients to talk openly about the death and their loss of the person. Staff support groups and staff meetings where feelings about loss of clients can be explored are very helpful. Whatever structures an agency devises, it is important to talk about the client's death and the loss and sadness felt by the workers who cared for that client. When workers are overcome with grief, they need to be given time off to sit with their feelings rather than rush on to the next piece of work.

When a chemically dependent client relapses, most workers ask themselves, "What else could I have done that might have made a difference? Did I screw up with this client?" Many of these are the same questions that get asked by the worker whose clients are dying, as irrational as that may sound. When clients in recovery from drug or alcohol abuse relapse, workers get angry. The countertransference reaction may be that "the client is making me look bad." It may be anger that the client allows him/herself to indulge in drugs while the worker has had to "renounce these infantile cravings" (Imhof et al., 1983). Compound the situation with an HIV involved client who relapses and the anger is increased. Practitioners working with PWAs sometimes get angry at how much beyond their control the client's deterioration is, or "How come I can't get him or her to do intrapsychic exploration?" "What's the sense of confronting denial, drinking, drugging, etc., since this person is going to die soon anyway?" Good work can only take place where there is common ground between the services the practitioner wants to provide and the services the client wishes to receive.

Anger prevents the worker from being empathic with the client. What many substance abuse professionals have done is to accept relapse as part of the disease of chemical dependency and, rather than being caught off guard and shocked by it, they plan for it and are prepared when it happens. A similar attitude must be maintained when a healthy PWA experiences a new or repeat opportunistic infection. Both situations are often outside of the locus of control of either client or worker.

Despite all the difficult emotions and countertransference reactions of workers in substance abuse and in AIDS it is possible for professionals to survive and thrive while doing this difficult and important work. It is also possible, although difficult, to remain centered and not burn out. It is crucial for workers to have support, both from clinical supervision and from their colleagues and peers. Both writers have also found their own psychotherapy to be extremely helpful in working through their own issues which lead to subjective countertransference. Time needs to be built in for grieving, mourning and for workers taking care of their own needs. Humor and lightheartedness are essential if one is to survive, hence all the AIDS jokes that AIDS services providers and PWAs tell each other. Questions of spirituality, the client's and the practitioner's, often arise during the course of treatment. Those workers who are involved in twelve-step self help groups like Alcoholics Anonymous find them to be an essential component of their support systems. Human service professionals must strive to take care of their own health and watch their own diet, exercise and assess their own intake of mood altering substances. They also need to put time aside to let the child in them come out and have fun now and then.

There are incredible rewards that come from working in AIDS or in substance abuse. The worker has the opportunity to evaluate the meaning and quality of his or her own life and work and establish true priorities. In the midst of the suffering, pain and sadness, an intensely intimate relationship often develops between the client and the worker that results from being allowed to accompany clients on their journeys in recovery or during the final phase of their lives. The intensity of the therapeutic relationship increases the pain felt by the worker when the client deteriorates and either relapses to drug use or dies of AIDS. One challenge for the professional is to learn how to tolerate all of these feelings, keep a professional objectivity, but not emotionally distance from the client. By not shutting down to these painful and sad feelings a tremendous benefit accrues to the worker that is carried over into a profoundly altered professional as well as personal life. The way one works with all clients is profoundly affected and enhanced by work with substance abusers and with people with HIV Spectrum Disease.

The writers have experienced a tremendous humbling of their own self-images through contact with clients. Creating a balance between the personal and professional spheres of one's life in response to the emotional demands of the work is critical but can be difficult when one's clients are getting AIDS and falling into the mire of drug use and one's friends are getting AIDS and falling into the mire of drug use. Working with two chronic, progressive diseases for which there are no cures and no vaccines and finding ways to instill hope in the clients and in ourselves is no easy task. And working with the gay or lesbian client who has multiple risks and complex issues around sex and drug use can test the worker's ability to work holistically, for one can't separate the issues into compartments, but must deal with the whole person all at once.

Professionals can make a major difference in helping clients to cope with pathology–be it AIDS or substance abuse related. We must learn not to judge our competence by what the outcome is for the client; we must judge our work by the quality of our skills and the depth of our caring. All individuals must choose their own paths and we have to be mature enough to allow our clients to live their lives as they need to and not necessarily as we would want them to. In this work we are sometimes fortunate enough to accompany a client on his or her chosen path toward growth, serenity, improved functioning and enhanced human relationships. At other times we are simply accompanying them through the chaos and pain of their existence. In either case our lives can become permanently enriched as a result of being along on the ride.

REFERENCES

Imhof, J., Hirsch, R., & Terenzi, R.E. (1983). Countertransferential and attitudinal considerations in the treatment of drug abuse and addiction. *The International Journal of the Addictions 18*(4), 491-510.

Luban, S. & Salon, R., 1981-84. Clinical Supervision, Van Etten Drug Treatment Program (discussions and seminars).

Macks, J. (1988). Women and AIDS: Countertransference issues. *Social Casework: AIDS–A Special Issue 69*, (6), 340-347.

National Institute on Drug Abuse Services Research Report. (1981). Comparative effectiveness of drug abuse treatment modalities (DHHS Publication No. ADM 81-1067) Washington, D.C.: U.S. Government Printing Office.

The pilot needle exchange study in New York City: a bridge to treatment, a report on the first ten months of operation. (1989). New York City Department of Health.

New York State Division of Substance Abuse Services (1989). Telephone conversation with Office of Communications.

Sorrell, S. (1990). Personal communication. Dr. Sorrell believes that approximately 50% or more of the clients in his methadone maintenance program at Roosevelt Hospital are using various drugs while in treatment. One third show positive urine toxicologies for substances of abuse, however he observes signs of abuse in about 20% of the patients whose urine tests are negative.

Spirituality in Everyday Life: Experiences of Gay Men of Alcoholics Anonymous

Robert J. Kus, RN, PhD

SUMMARY. Although gay American men are afflicted with alcoholism and other forms of chemical dependency at a much higher rate than their heterosexual brothers, many of them are experiencing fulfillment by living the spiritual way of life known as Alcoholics Anonymous.

To learn how gay men of AA go about doing spirituality in everyday life, 50 gay American men were interviewed in depth. The findings of this study are presented here so that clinicians can teach their gay male clients how other gay men recovering from chemical dependency go about practicing spirituality.

In everyday life, the men in this study practiced spirituality by maintaining sobriety, ridding themselves of internalized homophobia, communicating with their Higher Power (who was defined as God by the overwhelming majority of the study's participants), turning their lives and wills over to the care of God as they understood Him, performing good works (both corporal and spiritual works of mercy), meeting adult social roles, engaging in self-examination, applying AA slogans to everyday life, sharing themselves with others, attending AA meetings, seeking forgiveness, reading positive gay, alcoholic, and other literature, engaging in rituals,

---

Dr. Kus is a nurse-sociologist who specializes in gay men's studies and alcohol studies. Currently he's an associate professor in the College of Nursing at The University of Iowa. He is the editor of *Gay Men of Alcoholics Anonymous: Firsthand Accounts* (WinterStar Press, 1990) and *Keys to Caring: Assisting Your Gay & Lesbian Clients* (Alyson, 1990).

The author acknowledges the support of his research assistants who worked on this project: Zak Alder of Seattle; Steve Carlson of Iowa City; Douglas J. King of Chicago; and Bob Rowe of Oklahoma City.

49

engaging in sacrifice and discipline, and doing everyday tasks as well as they possibly could.

Tips on how clinicians may use this knowledge for their gay male clients are provided.

INTRODUCTION

"Ted" is a 26 year old bricklayer who does an honest day's work for an honest day's wages. Two years ago he was treated for alcoholism and cocaine addiction in an in-patient setting, and he has just received his 2-year chip from his AA group to commemorate two years of continuous sobriety. (A chip is a medallion commemorating an AA member's sobriety anniversary.)

In addition to attending one NA and two AA meetings every week, Ted makes coffee before meetings and helps to clean up after meetings by emptying ashtrays and straightening up chairs. He is always one of the first to offer newcomers a cheery greeting, and he sponsors two other men. He gives rides to meetings for persons who need it, volunteers at the intergroup AA office every Saturday morning answering the phone, and visits alcoholics who are in jail.

Ted lives alone with his dog Shambles whom he takes for a walk every day and, as he says, "spoils rotten." Although he used to attend a Protestant church in his little town, he hasn't attended regularly. In fact, he's known as a "holiday Christian," one who attends at Christmas and Easter, but rarely at other times. He still believes in and communicates with God.

As he continues in sobriety, he finds that he experiences more and more periods of serenity. He is also becoming more self-confident as he grows in sobriety, and he is able to set goals now. In fact, he has been accepted by a local university to study to become an R.N.; he would like eventually to counsel chemically dependent persons, especially gay men.

Shortly after he received his 2-year chip, one of the staff members from the inpatient treatment center where Ted received treatment asked Ted how he likes AA. He replied, "Oh, I can't tell you how much I owe to AA! In fact, it saved my life! I don't get the 'spiritual angle,' though. I guess I'm just not a very spiritual person."

Ted's response is most interesting as it reflects a lack of knowledge about what spirituality is and more than likely represents a confusion between "spirituality" and "religion." Ted's confusion is a common one. Many gay men of AA achieve great spiritual heights yet don't recognize their lives as spiritual, and many helping professionals also have a very fuzzy notion of what constitutes "spirituality" and how one can go about "doing spirituality." The counselor who realizes that spirituality consists not only of one's basic value system, but also of doing good works, could help Ted see that indeed he is living a spiritual life. Emptying ashtrays, walking his dog, sponsoring others, greeting newcomers, and the like are all examples of how Ted is living spiritually in everyday life.

Ted's knowledge deficit should, of course, be corrected, for AA is the primary path American alcoholics use to obtain sobriety, and AA is a spiritual form of treatment. Advising persons to live the AA program, while not understanding the concept of spirituality, is rather strange indeed. It is particularly important for helping professionals who work with gay men to be clear about spirituality for two reasons. First, gay American men are afflicted with alcoholism and other forms of chemical dependency at a very high rate of 20-42% (Fifield, 1975; Kelly, 1991; Lohrenz et al., 1978; Morales & Graves, 1983; Saghir & Robins, 1973). Recent research has shown that gay men in other societies too may be at greater risk for alcoholism than their heterosexual brothers. For example, Kus and Procházka (1991) have identified 22% of gay Czechoslovak men to be "definitely alcoholic," and another 6-15% of them have MAST test scores "suggestive of alcoholism." Second, many gay men have been alienated by anti-gay religious persons. Failing to distinguish religion from spirituality may be an obstacle for a man who has been hurt by such bigotry. Such a man may reject AA and other 12-step groups, thus diminishing his chances of a life of sobriety.

In this article, I will present how gay men of Alcoholics Anonymous defined spirituality and how they practiced it in their everyday lives. Armed with this knowledge, clinicians will better be able to teach gay men–and other types of clients too–what all is involved in spirituality. Clients can then use these spiritual skills with confidence in their recovery journeys without being confused about what spirituality is.

THE RESEARCH BASE

Information presented in this article was obtained from an in-depth interview type of research study conducted by the author with fifty (50) gay American men of Alcoholics Anonymous. The purpose of this study was to learn how gay American men of AA go about defining the concept of "spirituality," how they define and communicate with a Higher Power, and how they go about "doing spirituality" in everyday life.

FINDINGS AND DISCUSSION

The Concept of Spirituality

Although the men in this study had a difficult time defining spirituality in a concise way, they had no difficulty providing examples of what it covered. Likewise, they had no difficulty distinguishing spirituality from religion.

Spirituality was seen as something which every person has, unlike religion which only some people have. The men saw spirituality as the realm of life which deals with such things as one's basic values, behaviors which reflect one's basic value system, notions of good and evil, right or wrong, and the meaning of one's life. Most also saw spirituality as the realm of life which deals with the idea of God and afterlife. Behaviors included in spirituality will be discussed later in this article.

Religion was seen as more formal than spirituality and composed of formal doctrines, rituals, and hierarchies. The men in the study believed that all people are spiritual, but not all persons are religious. Further, while religion may help one become more spiritual, it does not necessarily work that way; one might be in a religion but have a poor spirituality, while another person may be very spiritual yet have no religion at all.

The clinician may teach the client about the distinction between religion and spirituality so the client does not become confused between the two and reject the 12-Step way of life, which is a spiritual program, if he is uncomfortable with religion.

Defining the Higher Power

In Alcoholics Anonymous, members learn quickly that they need to have some concept of God or a Higher Power, for many of the 12 Steps speak directly about God *"as we understood Him."*

In this study, the men defined the Higher Power in one of four ways. A few of the men had a very nebulous notion of a power greater than themselves but felt that there "must be something out there, sort of a force, a cosmic force, a superior intelligence." One man, who defined the higher power as himself, had a very difficult time discussing this issue with the researchers. Two men defined their higher power as their AA group.

The overwhelming majority of men, however, defined their higher power as God in the traditional sense, so that is the concept which this article will focus on. When first talking about God, many of the men referred to God as "He *or She,*" striving to use "politically correct" rhetoric even though none of them were Goddess worshipers. Once they had done this, they then spoke about God as He.

For most men, their childhood perception of God was that He was an old man with long, flowing hair sitting on a golden throne on a cloud surrounded by winged angels. The childhood view saw God as a vengeful creature who kept a list of one's wrongs while on Earth so He could punish the individual in the afterlife. Fortunately, in adulthood the men's views of God changed radically. When asked to describe their adult view of God, the men described God as loving, gentle, ever-merciful, gracious, always willing to listen and to help, a giver of gifts, the source of all joy, and a being who is very humorous. Although they acknowledged God to be all-powerful and the creator of the universe, most found it easier to see God as a personal friend. For many men, God was seen as their lover, a perfect lover. Many of the attributes the men saw in God were the same attributes they felt a good sponsor should possess, attributes such as willingness to listen, love and acceptance, forgiveness, help along the path of life, and the like.

Clinicians can help the gay man explore what he believes the higher power to be by asking such general questions as, "Tell me about your conception of a 'higher power," "What is this higher power like?'' ''What do you think the higher power's job description is?''

FINDINGS AND DISCUSSION: "DOING SPIRITUALITY IN EVERYDAY LIFE"

In this section, we explore how the men in this study went about "doing spirituality" in their everyday life. Clinicians can best help their gay clients live spiritually by sharing this information which was obtained from gay brothers in this study.

Maintaining Sobriety

Universally, the men felt maintaining sobriety was necessary for their spiritual life to develop. Without sobriety, one's spiritual life is usually neglected, one's higher power becomes alcohol and other mind-altering drugs, and one's self-centeredness leaves little room for practicing spirituality in everyday life.

Ridding Self of Internalized Homophobia

Internalized homophobia is the hatred of one's homosexuality. In early sobriety, virtually all gay men have internalized homophobia even though they often do not recognize this fact until after they have been sober for some time. The non-recognition is usually due to the fact that they have been anesthetizing their negative feelings with alcohol and other mind-altering drugs and are thus not able to recognize this negative feeling state. Because internalized homophobia is such a critical and universal block to spiritual progress in gay alcoholic men, it is important to consider its nature.

Internalized homophobia is characterized by feelings of inferiority, low self-esteem, shame at being gay, guilt, fear, anxiety, alcohol and other drug abuse, needing alcohol to have sex, homophobic reactions to gay brothers, passing as straight, and other negative feeling, thinking, and behaving states. In severe cases, internalized homophobia may lead to acute psychotic episodes and/or suicide.

Treatment for internalized homophobia in gay alcoholic men

involves: (1) maintaining sobriety; (2) getting to know as many positive gay men as possible; (3) doing positive gay reading; and (4) praying for acceptance of one's sexual orientation (Kus, 1987; 1990b). For the men in this study, the first four lines of the Serenity Prayer, "God grant me the serenity to accept the things I cannot change, courage to change the things I can, and the wisdom to know the difference," which is said at most AA meetings, was found to be very helpful. For example, what cannot be changed is one's alcoholism and one's sexual orientation; neither of these are chosen states. In terms of alcoholism, what can be changed is one's drinking; one does not have to drink. In terms of one's homosexuality, what can be changed is one's internalized homophobia; one can change his negative view and come to see being gay as positive rather than negative. One of the clearest signs of spiritual growth in a gay man of AA occurs when he begins to see his gay orientation as a divine gift for which to be thankful, rather than as a curse to be tolerated (Kus, 1988b).

Communicating with the Higher Power

The men talked both about how they communicated with God and how God then communicated with them. Communicating with God was done through three types of prayer.

The first kind of prayers were those of supplication, or asking. In childhood, the men said, this was their most common type of prayer. As children, they asked God mostly for material things such as a bicycle, toys, or a horse. In adulthood, however, they usually asked God for abstract things such as sobriety, serenity or a sense of peace, the knowledge of God's will for their lives, and the power to carry out God's will. Occasionally they did ask for material things such as financial help or a job, but usually they prayed for others such as their families, lovers, or ill friends.

The most common prayers offered to God in adulthood were those of thanksgiving. The men thanked God for such things as their sobriety, their lover if they had one, AA, jobs, health, and other blessings. Even if things were going poorly for a man, he would thank God for helping him cope, soberly, with whatever problems he had.

Finally, some men reported using cursing prayers in their pre-sobriety and early sobriety days. In this type of prayer, the gay man cursed God for having been created gay or for having been given alcoholism. Cursing prayers disappeared as the men grew in sobriety and as their internalized homophobia diminished.

The men talked also about how God communicates to them. Mostly, they saw God communicating with them through other people, such as their sponsors or fellow AA members, and though literature which helped them grow. Some experienced God by feelings of intense peace while meditating. In fact, many defined prayer as "me talking to God" and meditation as "God talking to me." God also made His presence known by showering the men with personal gifts such as sobriety and friends and general gifts such as flowers and trees and the other beautiful things of nature. Some men had peak experiences, which Maslow (1962, 1964) defines as "transient moments of self-actualization." These experiences can also be seen as periods of intense ecstasy or joy. One man talked about having a peak experience while he was acting on stage.

> There came a moment when I no longer was an actor. God was acting through me. I was just a vehicle for God's work. It was an incredible experience like no other I had ever experienced. What I was doing was far beyond my capabilities; God was truly working through me.

Finally, some felt that God spoke directly to them. One of the most interesting stories was told by this man:

> I was in bar and pretty drunk. As I was standing at a urinal, a voice came to me and said, "You don't have to live this way." I went home shortly after that, and when I woke up in the morning, I remembered that voice. I also remember having seen an advertisement on the L train the night before saying, "If you are gay and have a drinking problem, call this number." I called that number, joined AA, and have not had a drink since.

Turning One's Will and Life Over to the Care of God

The Third Step of AA states, "(We) Made a decision to turn our will and our lives over to the care of God *as we understood Him.*" As part of living spiritually, the men in this study also turned their wills and lives over to the care of God. When asked how they knew what was God's will versus their own will, most men said that when something was God's will, they felt good, or peaceful, inside. When something was not God's will, they would often experience negative feelings, thoughts, or behaviors. For example, something which was not in God's plan for them would often lead them to experience feelings such as anxiety, "stinking thinking" which includes self-pity and the inability to concentrate on every-day tasks, and behaviors such as getting angry at others with little provocation. Because the 11th Step says, in part, to pray "only for knowledge of His will for us and the power to carry that out," most of the men did ask God to show them His will for them in everyday life.

Doing Good Works

The good works which the men did in everyday life were divided into two types: corporal works of mercy and spiritual works of mercy.

Corporal works of mercy are those acts which are designed to help meet the physical needs of others. Examples of these activities would be caring for animals, making coffee for fellow AA members at meetings, giving food to the homeless, providing rides to AA meetings, or donating clothes to organizations such as the Salvation Army or St. Vincent de Paul Society.

Spiritual works of mercy include visiting the sick, listening to others in need, counseling, and visiting the imprisoned. Many of the good works done by the men came about as a result of living AA. For example, as a gay man's internalized homophobia was replaced by a feeling of gay pride, he often found himself wondering what he was doing to be a solid citizen in the gay men's community. This would often lead him to engage in activities to help gay brothers such as volunteering for gay crisis centers, visiting brothers sick with AIDS in their homes or hospitals, volunteering for hospice organizations, or volunteering for gay organizations.

Meeting Adult Social Roles

Spirituality is reflected in how well we carry out our basic adult responsibilities, according to the men in this study. A spiritual man does his job well, pays his bills on time, meets the responsibilities of couplehood if he is coupled, takes care of his home, meets the responsibilities of parenthood if he is a father, and engages in good citizenship. According to the men in this study, a person who is not following a spiritual path very closely will tend to neglect the responsibilities of his basic adult social roles or to "cut corners" to get by with doing the minimum.

Living an Examined Life

To grow spiritually, one must live an examined life. An "examined life" refers to paying attention to how one is living life. In AA, the Fourth Step calls for members to make "a searching and fearless moral inventory" of themselves. The men in this study reported that in doing this Step, they not only identified their shortcomings or "character defects," but they also identified their strengths. In addition to identifying what any alcoholic might have on such a list, they also identified gay-specific items such as internalized homophobia, rude behavior towards other gay men, or unsafe sex while drunk.

The AA Tenth Step, "Continued to take personal inventory and when we were wrong promptly admitted it," was often done on a daily basis. Some men reported that they pretty much continually did a Tenth Step all through the day, while others reported they set aside a special time each day, usually right before bedtime, to reflect on their day to see how they did. Many men shared that often when a day is becoming unbearable or they are becoming "out of sorts," they need to do a quick Tenth Step to see what is going wrong. Only by identifying the source of their discomfort could they then take measures to counteract the discomfort.

Sharing Self with Others

The men in this study held the traditional Western civilization notion about self-disclosure; that is, that sharing one's self is very important to one's well-being. The late Sidney Jourard (1971), who devoted his life to the study of self-disclosure and its effects on health, felt that most illnesses in this world were due to individuals not sharing themselves with others. By keeping things bottled up, especially negative things, one can experience such physical illnesses as ulcers or heart attacks, mental or emotional illnesses such as depression or anxiety states, or spiritual illnesses such as feelings of meaninglessness and hopelessness. The men felt that without sharing themselves with others, they would be heading for a relapse, and relapse can lead to death. Therefore, sharing of one's self is literally a matter of life and death. Two sayings provided by some of the men stressing the importance of sharing of self were, "A problem shared is a problem halved; while a problem kept secret is a problem doubled" and "You are as sick as your secrets."

In the AA context, sharing of self is done while attending AA meetings, in doing certain of the 12 Steps, in particular Steps Five (admitting to God, self, and another human being the exact nature of one's wrongs), Step Nine (making direct amends to persons one has harmed unless to do so would injure them or others), and part of Step Twelve (carrying the AA message to alcoholics), and in speaking to one's sponsor. Friends, especially those new-found AA friends, were found to be very helpful to the men in their sobriety journeys (Kus, 1991).

Attending AA Meetings

Although attending AA meetings is not a requirement for membership in AA and is not one of the 12 Steps, all of the men reported that attending meetings helped them grow spiritually. In meetings, they were able to hear messages from their Higher Power which were spoken through the members. From meetings, they were able to put their own problems into proper perspective and develop a sense of humor, a key element of a healthy spirituality.

The pre and post meeting gatherings, as well as AA gatherings, were likewise important to the men in their spiritual journeys. In Chicago, for example, the gay men of AA often frequented the back room of a local restaurant. Almost any time of day or night a man could find gay AA brothers with whom he could share. I suspect that an incredible amount of growth is done in such pre and post meeting AA gatherings.

Seeking Forgiveness

When individuals violate their moral code, they experience guilt. On the one had, guilt is good; it not only shows that we have a conscience, but it helps keep us in line. On the other had, unresolved guilt may lead to low self-esteem and spiritual distress. Therefore, a healthy spirituality will provide a way for reducing one's guilt. Seeking forgiveness is the most common way to relieve guilt, and AA provides specific ways to help individuals do this.

After becoming ready to have God remove one's "defects of character" in Step Six, in Step Seven one actually asks God to remove one's "shortcomings." In Step Eight, one makes a list of persons he has harmed, and in Step Nine makes direct amends to the people on the list unless to do so would injure them or others. The men in this sample found that seeking forgiveness was relatively easy from God, not too difficult from others, but very difficult from themselves. "I'm my own worst enemy" was often shared by the men. Although they could easily forgive others, they had a hard time forgiving themselves. May figured out that they had harmed themselves more then anyone else by their drinking. As a result of this insight, they came to place themselves on the top of their Step Eight list, and when doing Step Nine, they tried to make amends to themselves and forgive themselves for past mistakes. Virtually all men in the study felt that being gentle with themselves would be a lifelong task.

Doing Bibliotherapy

Bibliotherapy may be defined as "the use of literature of any type, and in any form, for the purpose of self-help or personal growth" (Kus, 1989). "Of any type" means that any literature, even comic books, could be therapeutic if used for personal growth and self-help. "In any form" means that the literature could be on audio-tapes for the illiterate or blind person.

All of the men in the study used bibliotherapy as part of their spiritual program. Literature which was particularly helpful were meditation guides such as Hazelden's *Touchstones: A book of daily meditations for men* (1986), and AA literature such as *Alcoholics Anonymous (3rd ed.)* (1976), commonly known as the Big Book. Two books which were seen as particularly helpful for treating the gay man's internalized homophobia were *Reflections of a rock lobster: A story of growing up gay* (Fricke, 1981) and *The best little boy in the world* (Reid, 1973). Gay related books on alcoholism were very helpful for many men. Literature in this category includes academically-oriented books such as Finnegan and McNally's (1987) *Dual identities: Counseling chemically dependent gay men and lesbians;* Ziebold and Monegon's (1985) *Gay and sober: Directions for counseling and therapy;* and Kominars' (1989) *Accepting ourselves: The 12-step journey of recovery from addictions for gay men and lesbians;* light reading pamphlets such as John Michael's (1976 and 1977) *The gay drinking problem: There is a solution* and *Sober, clean and gay!* and autobiographies such as the Gay Council on Drinking Behavior's (1981-2) *The way back: The stories of gay and lesbian alcoholics* and the book edited by Kus (1990a) titled *Gay men of Alcoholics Anonymous: First-hand accounts.*

Performing Rituals

Many men in this study reported engaging in certain rituals to express their spirituality. For example, some lit candles or incense while meditating. Those who had a religion practiced the rituals of the religion. A Jewish man might host a Passover Seder while the Catholic or Protestant man might decorate a Christmas tree, attend services, and receive communion, and the pagan man might celebrate Winter Solstice.

Sacrificing and Being Disciplined

In virtually every religious and spiritual tradition, there is the idea that to allow the spirit to grow, we must practice sacrifice and discipline on our bodies. Some of the sacrifices and forms of discipline the men discussed doing as part of their spirituality were fasting, going without luxuries and giving the money to the poor, doing without sleep to stay with a friend in need, listening when they would rather be talking, keeping quiet about others' faults when they would have preferred to confront the offending person, doing a good job at work when they would rather have been sloughing off, and refraining from gossiping when they were anxious to do so.

Doing Everyday Tasks as Well as One Can

In the late 19th Century, there lived in France a Discalced Carmelite nun by the name of Therese Martin who talked about "the little way." This "little way" referred to doing everyday tasks, no matter how small or trivial, in the best way one could. Although she died at the age of 24, her "little way" made Therese a saint, one of the most popular saints of our times.

The men in this study also often talked about doing everyday tasks as well as they could. Because a man never does everything as well as he could, each day is always a new challenge, and there is always work to do on one's spiritual journey.

CONCLUSION

In this study of gay recovering alcoholic men, we saw that most of the sample defined their higher power as God. The men distinguished the concept of "spirituality," which everyone has, from "religion," which only some people have. This finding is very important, for many gay men have been alienated by anti-gay religious persons. As a result, *some* gay men have simply abandoned their religious heritage and want nothing to do with organized religion. If they had not been able to distinguish religion from spirituality, they may have rejected AA (a spiritual, non-religious program) and thus would have not been able to maintain sobriety and experience spiritual growth in the AA context.

In order to progress on their spiritual journey, the men felt that they had to maintain sobriety. In everyday life, the men expressed their spirituality by taking steps to rid themselves of internalized homophobia; communicating with the higher power through prayer and meditation; turning over their wills and lives to the care of God as they understood Him; doing good works; engaging in self-examination; applying common AA slogans to their lives; sharing themselves with others; attending AA meetings; seeking forgiveness; doing positive readings; engaging in rituals; doing sacrifice and discipline; and doing everyday tasks as well as they could.

CLINICAL IMPLICATIONS

This study has many implications for clinicians who work with gay recovering alcoholic men.

First, clinicians may help clear up misconceptions the gay man might have about spirituality versus religion. The young man at the beginning of this article, for example, thought he was not very spiritual even though he was living a very spiritual life. He had spirituality confused with religion. This is a common misconception. This is particularly important for many gay men to know because they may have been treated in a very unspiritual-like manner by homophobic men and women of the clergy. Such behavior sometimes leads gay men to become anti-religious, at least for a period of time, and the anti-gay bigotry they experience from the clergy may even lead the man to become angry at God and develop feelings of estrangement from God.

Second, the clinician should help the gay man overcome any internalized homophobia he has, keeping in mind that in the early days of sobriety, some gay men do not recognize that they have it. I have found it helpful to ask gay men "On a scale of 0-9, with 0 meaning hating being gay, and 9 meaning loving being gay, where would you put yourself right now." This often provides some indication as to the level of internalized homophobia the man has. Once the internalized homophobia has been identified, the clinician may help the man rid himself of it by the strategies already listed: sobriety; making positive gay friends; reading positive gay literature; and praying for acceptance.

Sometimes, gay men in early sobriety will say, "Oh, I accept being gay just fine. I have to keep it very hidden, though, because everybody else will reject me." This individual often misses out on help he could receive from AA because he does not share his life with the other AA members for fear of rejection if they learn he is gay. In most instances, from my research and clinical practice, I have found that one's fear of rejection is directly related to one's internalized homophobia. A truly homophobic gay man would have trouble functioning happily in the Castro area of San Francisco (a gay Mecca), while a man with little or no internalized homophobia can function happily in even the smallest of communities in the most remote and redneck places in America.

Clinicians should also remember that how a gay man communicates with God about his homosexuality is sometimes a good indicator of his internalized homophobia level. The man afflicted with internalized homophobia is not likely to be thanking God for having created him gay. Instead of seeing his sexual orientation as a divine gift, he sees it as a curse.

A word of caution is in order. Clinicians should never force a gay man to disclose his gay identity to others; this is his, and only his, decision. However, the clinician may provide support if the client decides to disclose.

Third, the clinician may help the gay man explore various conceptions of a higher power. The professional should reassure the gay man that often one's conception of God changes over time, and that from this study, men came to define God in a much more loving, gentle way as they grew in spirituality.

Fourth, the clinician may help the gay man pray. At first in sobriety, the man may need to rely exclusively on formal prayers such as The Lord's Prayer which Jesus taught or the first four lines of the Serenity Prayer which are commonly said at AA meetings. Or, the clinician may teach the man how to create his own very simple prayers such as, "Help!" or "Thanks!"

Fifth, the clinician should be able to teach the gay client how other gay men go about "doing" spirituality in everyday life. This would be a very worthwhile project since many gay men, like other people, often don't associate walking their dog, being kind to others, and paying their bills as ways of doing spirituality.

Finally, giving the client positive strokes for his spiritual efforts helps him on his journey.

REFERENCES

Alcoholics Anonymous. (1976). *Alcoholics Anonymous* (3rd ed.). New York: AA World Services, Inc.

Fifield, L. (1975). *On my way to nowhere: Alienated, isolated, drunk.* Los Angeles: Gay Community Services Center & Department of Health Services.

Finnegan, D.G., & McNally, E.B. (1987). *Dual identities: Counseling chemically dependent gay men and lesbians.* Center City, MN: Hazelden.

Fricke, A. (1981). *Reflections of a rock lobster: A story of growing up gay.* Boston: Alyson.

Gay Council on Drinking Behavior. (1981-1982). *The way back: The stories of gay and lesbian alcoholics* (2nd ed.). Washington, D.C.: Whitman-Walker Clinic.

Hazelden. (1986). Touchstones: A book of daily meditations for men. Center City, MN: Hazelden.

Johnson, V.E. (1980). *I'll quit tomorrow: A practical guide to alcoholism treatment.* San Francisco: Harper & Row, Pub., Inc.

Jourard, S.M. (1971). *The transparent self* (Rev. Ed.). New York: D. Van Nostrand Reinhold Co., Inc.

Kelly, J. (1991). *San Francisco lesbian, gay and bisexual alcohol and other drug needs assessment study: Vol. 1.* Sacramento, CA: EMT Associates, Inc.

Kominars, S. (1989). *Accepting ourselves: The 12-step journey of recovery from addictions for gay men and lesbians.* San Francisco: Harper & Row, Pub., Inc.

Kus, R.J. (1987). Gay consultations in non-gay treatment settings. *Professional Counselor* July / August, 46-55.

Kus, R.J. (1988a). "Working the program:" The Alcoholics Anonymous experience and gay American men. *Holistic Nursing Practice.* 2(4), 62-74.

Kus, R.J. (1988b). Alcoholism and non-acceptance of gay self: The critical link. *Journal of Homosexuality, 15,* 25-41.

Kus, R.J. (1989). Bibliotherapy and gay American men of Alcoholics Anonymous. *Journal of Gay & Lesbian Psychotherapy, 1* (2), 73-86.

Kus, R.J. (Ed.) (1990a). *Gay men of Alcoholics Anonymous: First-hand accounts.* North Liberty, IA: WinterStar Press.

Kus, R.J. (1990b). Alcoholism in the gay and lesbian communities. In R.J. Kus (Ed.), *Keys to caring: Assisting your gay and lesbian clients* (pp. 66-81). Boston: Alyson.

Kus, R.J. (1991). Sobriety, friends, and gay men. *Archives of Psychiatric Nursing, 5*(3), June, pp. 171-177.

Kus, R.J. & Procházka, I. (1991, June). *Alcoholism in gay Czechoslovak men: An incidence study.* Paper presented at the 36th International Institute on the Prevention & Treatment of Alcoholism, Stockholm, Sweden.

Lohrenz, L., Connelly, J., Coyne, L., & Spare, K. (1978). Alcohol problems in several midwestern homosexual communities. *Journal of Alcohol Studies, 39,* 1959-1963.

Maslow, A.H. (1962). *Toward a psychology of being.* Princeton, NJ: Van Nostrand Reinhold Co., Inc.

Maslow, A.H. (1964). *Religions, values and peak experiences.* Columbus, Ohio: The Ohio State University Press.

Michael J. (1976). *The gay drinking problem . . . there is a solution.* Minneapolis: CompCare.

Michael, J. (1977). *Sober, clean, and gay.* Minneapolis: CompCare.

Morales, E.S., & Graves, M.A. (1983). *Substance abuse: Patterns and barriers to treatment for gay men and lesbians in San Francisco.* San Francisco: San Francisco Prevention Resources Center.

Reid, J. (1973). *The best little boy in the world.* New York: Ballantine.

Saghir, M., & Robins, E. (1973). *Male and female homosexuality.* Baltimore: Williams & Wilkins.

Ziebold, T.O., & Monegon, J.E. (Eds.) (1985). *Gay and Sober: Directions for counseling and therapy.* New York: Harrington Park Press.

Chemical Dependency
in Gay and Lesbian Youth

Francine Shifrin, CSW
Mirtha Solis, CSW

The high incidence of chemical dependency among the adult lesbian and gay population has been noted by several authors (Falco, 1991; Lewis & Jordan, 1989; Nardi, 1982). However, very little information exists concerning chemical dependency problems among gay youth. The lack of attention to this population reflects the assumption that the youth's homosexual or lesbian identity is a precursor to a normal heterosexual object choice or is a maladaptive pattern. Up until recently, the gay youth has had to face the denial of his or her heterosexually oriented family and educational systems, as well as exclusion from the adult lesbian and gay culture. In this article, we will briefly describe the chemical dependency problems among a population of youths drawn from the Hetrick-Martin Institute and outline recommendations for treating these youths in both a gay-identified and a traditional treatment setting.

The Hetrick-Martin Institute is a multiservice agency which offers gay and lesbian youth counseling, socialization and educational services. In addition, the agency operates an outreach program for homeless gay and lesbian youth. Data on the chemical dependency problems of the youth in both programs was collected. Counselors were asked to rate their clients' use of substances based on information compiled in an intake interview and on chart notes. In the

Francine Shifrin is Director of Substance Abuse Services at Covenant House and is also in private practice in New York City.

Mirtha Solis is Assistant Director of Outreach House and is also in private practice in Queens, New York.

counseling program data was collected on 191 males and 75 females. For the males 17% reported frequent usage and 19% reported usage in which symptoms of chemical dependency were present. The mean age for males was 20 years. For the females 18% reported frequent usage whereas 17% reported problematic usage. The mean age was 19 years old. Frequent usage was defined as 3-4 times a month. The three most commonly used and abused substances were alcohol, marijuana, and cocaine. The majority of the clients presented a picture of polysubstance abuse with marijuana and alcohol as the two most frequently used substances.

In our outreach program to homeless youth a very different pattern of chemical dependency emerged. Out of the seventy-five clients who have had an intake at the storefront, all of them are addicted to crack. All except two were male.

Because this data was based on self-report it is likely that drug and alcohol usage has been underreported by the youth in the counseling program. Even though the counselors were given objective criteria on which to base their rating, no measure of reliability had been included in this study. Our sample of females was small and less representative of the general population of adolescent lesbians. It should be noted that originally Hetrick and Martin reported chemical dependency problems in 9% of the agency's population in the counseling and socialization programs (Hetrick and Martin, 1987). Since that original work, the intake has been modified to include a more extensive drug and alcohol assessment that is more sensitive to detecting the frequency of symptomatology.

Our research is at a beginning stage. Obviously much more work with gay youth and their patterns of substance abuse needs to be done. This initial study seems to demonstrate that alcohol and marijuana are very much a part of the gay youth's experience. Over a third of this population has frequent or problematic usage putting them at high risk for chemical dependency problems in adulthood. This suggests that the high incidence of chemical dependency among gays and lesbians may begin in adolescence. Lastly, the gay youth's use of substances had serious implications for the practice of safer sex techniques which is already problematic in this population.

Before proceeding to a discussion of treatment we would like to briefly describe the issues that underlie the gay youth's use of chemicals. As many authors have stated, the development of a homosexual or gay identity occurs in the context of stigma (Martin, 1982; Troiden, 1989). Prior to adolescence, the gay or lesbian adolescent has a "sense of being different" from his or her peers (Minton and McDonald, 1984). As homosexual impulses emerge, the youth begins to associate these previous feelings of being different with sexuality (Troiden, 1989). As children, homosexual youth have been exposed to the homophobia of the larger culture. During adolescence they realize that these feelings will place them in a devalued group (Hetrick and Martin, 1987).

This stigmatized role produces hiding and isolation, maladaptive sexual patterns and attempts to change one's orientation (Hetrick & Martin, 1987; Martin, 1982; Troiden,1989). Thus alcohol and drug usage for the lesbian and gay youth is multifunctional: it medicates the anxiety caused by the need to conceal one's identity; helps to discharge sexual impulses more comfortably; decreases the depression and dissonance that is generated by the adolescent's discovery of his or her sexual identity; acts as an antidote to the pain of exclusion, ridicule and rejection of the family and peer group; provides a feeling of power and self-worth to counteract the youth's sense of being devalued; and offers a sense of identity, wholeness and a soothing that is missing in his or her daily experience.

In the context of development, adolescence is the second separation-individuation process with many tasks. Much like the toddler, the adolescent ventures out into the world to master new challenges and relationships utilizing these experiences to develop his or her sense of self. Most often the gay youth is estranged from family members and is confronted with a hostile environment. Thus this break in parental support and the lack of appropriate peer and adult interactions predisposes the lesbian or homosexual youth to use substances to manage these developmental tasks. The substances become transitional objects that offer support, mastery, and a feeling of wholeness.

Although some research has refuted the importance of the gay bar in the development of adult alcoholism (Kus, 1988), it does remain a place to feel safe, to socialize and to find partners. For the gay youth, as for any youth, bars are associated with adulthood, adventure and a sense of belonging. The lack of structured activities for the gay youth makes the influence of bars an important factor. According to the research on adolescent group affiliation and drug and alcohol use, those youth involved in formal goal directed groups "demonstrated less substance abuse than those involved in informal associations" (Selnow & Crano, 1986). Therefore, the lack of structured settings and the norms of the bar culture that reinforce substance abuse would seem to be potent predisposing factors. In regard to gay homeless youth, crack is an integral part of the street life. It is the glue that holds the system together. Oftentimes the young hustler must be high to perform sex acts with the John. The Johns may pay the youth in crack which insures the possibility of more sex. If the young person has a pimp, it is in the pimp's best interest to keep the hustler addicted.

In our discussion of treatment we will examine the following issues: prevention, gay youth in a straight treatment setting, the role of the family in treatment, and the factors that we have encountered in our own experience.

In a consideration of prevention the utilization of a sociocultural model of chemical dependency emphasizes the importance of decreasing homophobia in society. That is, chemical dependency as a symptom of oppression (Nardi, 1982) can be lessened through a legal and societal validation of a gay and lesbian lifestyle. For the gay or lesbian adolescent, this loosening of oppression would obliterate the need to conceal his or her sexual identity and insure that he or she would have role models, family and friends to assist in the process of accepting and integrating their sexual orientation.

Moving from a broad sociocultural perspective to specific institutions and interventions, the educational system is an integral part of adolescent life. Within this system a gay positive environment needs to be created. One way to create such an environment is to present accurate information on sexual identity. This could take the form of posters, flyers and literature in public areas, guidance offices and the school library. The guidance counselor or school social worker who places a pamphlet on gay and lesbian issues in a common area with other literature gives the adolescent a positive message and allows him or her to discuss sexual issues when and if the youth is ready to do so. Another part of this work is to include the gay and lesbian life-style in academic coursework. Gay sexuality should be presented in health courses as a valid, healthy expression of sexuality. History and current events classes should contain information on the gay life-style. Finally the development of a multicultural curricula that includes gays and lesbians as a minority should be part of the educational system's efforts to counteract prejudice.

Most educational systems have drug/alcohol prevention programs as part of their curricula. It is evident that oppression and other social stressors predispose a young person to alcohol and drug usage. In order to deal effectively with the concerns of gay or lesbian adolescents, prevention efforts need to include group programming that provides support and assistance in the development of a positive gay identity. This type of intervention is not limited to gay youth and needs to be implemented in any school system that contains minority youth.

Any type of special programming should include activities within the school that are gay focused–for example in New York City a trip to the Lesbian Herstory Archives or simply posting a listing of gay youth organizations that are present within the community. The formation of a separate gay and lesbian student group that can sponsor activities would be appropriate in larger schools that have many clubs.

Preventive efforts need to include the adult gay community. In an area like New York City which has a large lesbian and gay community there are only three organizations that serve gay youth. The gay community can and should take more responsibility for organizing activities that focus on youth. This becomes especially important in more suburban areas where role models are less available. The gay community seems to be resistant to reaching out to youth because of its fear of confronting the societal perception of homosexuals as pederasts. Since one of the common myths about homosexuals and lesbians is that they will seek out younger people, many men and women are afraid that if they do reach out to youth, their actions will be interpreted as emanating from sexual desire. The early experiences of the founders of the Hetrick-Martin Institute illustrate how these stereotypes inhibit adult participation in the welfare of gay youth. When Damien Martin and Emery Hetrick were trying to start an advocacy group for youth, many professionals did not want to get involved for fear they would jeopardize their professional reputation. In exhibiting this resistance, the gay community has given silent acquiescence to this stereotype.

Another major component of treatment is the issue of gay youth in straight treatment settings. Since the gay youth will represent a minority in such a setting, he or she can easily emerge as a vehicle for diverting the group's attention. This pattern of scapegoating may take many forms involving the staff and the active participation of the gay client (Wellisch, DeAngelis and Bond, 1979). Thus the client's gayness becomes the primary focus of the treatment to the exclusion of other themes and maladaptive behavior.

In such a setting the youth may utilize cross-dressing or violating the norms of gender appropriate behavior as "a way of testing limits" (Wellisch, DeAngelis & Bond, 1979). That is, if a youth senses others discomfort with his or her homosexuality, he or she will use it to enrage the staff and repeat the familiar patterns of rejection, failure and self-negation. The staff must be alert to this as a defensive maneuver and attempt to treat the underlying pain and self-hatred.

It should be anticipated that there will be friction and hostility between gay and non-gay clients. Each group will be resistant to identifying with the feelings, situations and conflicts of the other for fear it will mean that they are like the other group (Wellisch, DeAngelis and Bond, 1979). As previously noted, the staff must appropriately interpret the hostility and underlying resistance.

If within the treatment setting there are special interest groups, then a lesbian or gay male or mixed group can be established. However, if no such structure exists, the formation of a group for gays and lesbians may serve to promote defensiveness, scapegoating and isolation within the setting and thus be contraindicated.

All staff should receive training in gay life-style issues and should not manifest any homophobia. Ideally, there should be some openly gay and lesbian staff members as role models. In addition, there should be a gay sensitive environment that contains posters, literature, movies and general information that speaks directly to the gay life-style and specific issues of chemically dependent gay people.

The third treatment issue we would like to address is the role of the family in treatment. The family's involvement in treatment is crucial to the adolescent's recovery. Although this statement can be made with any chemically dependent individual, we believe it is even more crucial in dealing with the adolescent chemically dependent client because of his or her struggle for identity and the family system's adjustment to these changes. As the recovering adolescent attempts to assume more responsibilities and separate activities, these shifts bring a certain degree of chaos to the family system and provoke the family system's resistance to change.

In the family treatment of gay youth, disclosure of one's sexual identity will be a prominent feature. Unlike their adult counterparts, the youth's disclosure is beset by problems related to their economic and physical dependence. Thus, each case must be assessed carefully and, in a great many instances, disclosure of the youth's sexuality is not advisable.

Thus, counseling should be directed towards exploring with the youth his or her parent's attitudes towards homosexuality or lesbianism and their possible reactions should the youth decide to reveal his/her sexuality. For example:

Social Worker:	Have your parents ever said anything about gay people?
Client:	No, not really.
S.W.:	How about when they read about gay protests or see TV shows with a gay theme?
Client:	My father thinks that the people who demonstrated outside Saint Patrick's Cathedral are not really Catholics. He said, you couldn't be a homosexual, a sinner and a religious person.
S.W.:	So, it sounds like your father thinks homosexuality is a sin?
Client:	Yeah, I think he does.

In anticipating the parent's reaction, a role play in which the client plays one or both parents might be helpful in reaching a decision regarding whether or not to self disclose. In some cases the youth's desire to tell his parents, peers or siblings will represent a desire to sabotage treatment. In all cases the youth needs to know that confidentiality will be respected, that the staff will not divulge the youth's sexual orientation and, that his or her sexual identity can be addressed in a safe therapeutic environment that endorses the client's control over this information. Family treatment should contain a didactic as well as a dynamic component. Family members may possess a great deal of distorted information about lesbianism and homosexuality. For example, it was commonly believed the homosexuality caused alcoholism. The family must be given clear, accurate gay-positive information so that appropriate focus on the problem of chemical dependency can be maintained.

The family's handling of the youth's sexual orientation must be explored. However, this work must not be done at the expense of ignoring the other family dynamics. These families, as in all families with a chemically dependent member, will vary in the degree and type of dysfunction displayed. Often, in these families the members' focus on the client's sexual identity diverts attention from other themes and dynamics. It should be noted that, like their heterosexual counterparts, these clients are more likely to have substance abusing family members, an issue which must be addressed in treatment and counseling sessions.

The case of a 19 year old lesbian illustrates a family's chemical dependency and underlying psychopathology. Both of Mary's parents were chemically dependent; her father dealt drugs and was incarcerated for most of her childhood. All, except one of her three sisters, abuse drugs and alcohol. As with children of alcoholics, Mary fell into the role of caretaker in a chaotic, often unpredictable environment. She felt different from the other girls from childhood on, and during adolescence attached this difference to her lesbianism. She tried to deny her sexuality by getting pregnant and engaged in self-destructive behavior including drug and alcohol usage to medicate her anxiety, loneliness and depression. When the family discovered her lesbianism, her father raped her, as he stated, "to teach her how to be a real woman" and attempted to have sexual relations with her on one or two other occasions. Thus, her lesbianism became the smoke screen for the family's underlying pathology.

In terms of our own experience, problems we encounter with young gay substance abusers reflect the denial inherent in chemical dependency, as well as the impact of the lack of resources and gay-sensitive treatment facilities. Resistance to admitting a problem exists with chemical dependency is not uncommon among substance abusers. Denial often exists at many levels–the individual, the family, the community. Because of the lack of gay-sensitive programs for these teenagers, at times even social service providers fall into the trap of thinking that maybe the substance abuse is not significant or that it may just be a phase that the adolescent will overcome on his or her own. Gay and lesbian social service providers may, at times, be oversensitive to the discrimination and lack of understanding that exist in most treatment facilities and avoid sending a young person for treatment. However, this allows treatment programs to continue on the path of discrimination and ignorance of homosexuality and to avoid the special issues and needs of lesbian and gay adolescents in recovery.

In conclusion, clearly much more research needs to be done to draw any conclusions about the chemical dependency problems of gay and lesbian adolescents. Our work suggests several ideas for future inquiry. First, can these rates be replicated utilizing a greater number of cases and how do these rates compare to a broader spectrum of gay and lesbian adolescents, e.g., those who are involved in non-counseling situations or those in more rural communities. The study of gender and gender identity is another area of great concern. One would expect that a more positive gay identity would affect the rate of chemical dependency. Lastly, the role of ethnicity would seem to be a strong variable as it is in heterosexual adolescents (Kinney, 1991).

A better understanding of chemical dependency among gay and lesbian youth can inform prevention and treatment programs. Even without further inquiry, there are actions that can be taken. The issue of visibility cuts across both prevention and treatment. There needs to be a much greater recognition that gay and lesbian adolescents exist and that homophobia can contribute to the development of chemical dependency problems.

In regard to prevention, the creation of more gay positive alternatives for socialization and activities that the adolescent can use to foster a healthy sense of self (e.g., clubs, hobbies, sports) will reduce the likelihood of the development of substance abuse problems. In either area of treatment or prevention we believe that the needs of the gay and lesbian adolescent will be best served by both exclusively gay and lesbian focused institutions like the Hetrick-Martin Institute as well as by traditional institutions of the larger culture modified to convey a sense of inclusion.

REFERENCES

Falco, K. (1991). *Psychotherapy with Lesbian Clients* New York: Brunner/Mazel, Inc.

Hetrick, E., & Martin, A.D. (1987). Developmental issues and their resolution for gay and lesbian adolescents. *Journal of Homosexuality, 14,* 26-44.

Kinney, J. (1991). Adolescence. In J. Kinney (Ed.) *Clinical Manual of Substance Abuse* (pp. 208-223) St. Louis: Mosby-Year Book.

Kus, R. (1988). Alcoholism and non acceptance of gay self: The Critical link. In M. Ross (Ed.), *The Treatment of homosexuality with mental health disorders* (pp. 24-40). New York: The Haworth Press, Inc.

Lewis, R. and Jordan, S. (1989). Treatment of the Gay or Lesbian Alcoholic. In Lawson, G. and Lawson, A. (Eds.) *Alcoholism and Substance Abuse in Special Populations.* (pp. 165-203). Rockville, Maryland: Aspen Press.

Martin, A.D. (1982). Learning to hide: The socialization of the gay adolescent. *Adolescent Psychiatry: Developmental and Clinical Studies, 10,* 52-65.

Minton, A., & McDonald, G. (1984). Homosexual identity formation as a developmental process. *Journal of Homosexuality, 9,* 99-103.

Mongeon, J. ,& Ziebold, T. (1982). Preventing alcohol abuse in the gay community: toward a theory and a model. *Journal of Homosexuality, 7,* 89-100.

Nardi, P. (1982). Alcoholism and homosexuality: A theoretical perspective. *Journal of Homosexuality, 4,* 9-23.

Selnow, G. , & Crano, W. (1986). Formal vs. informal group affiliations: Implication for alcohol and drug use among adolescents. *Journal of Studies on Alcohol, 47,* 48-52.

Troiden, R. (1989). The formation of homosexual identities. In G. Herdt (Ed.), *Gay and Lesbian Youth* (pp. 43-73). New York: Harrington Park Press.

Wellisch, D., DeAngelis, G., & Bond, M. (1979). Family treatment of the homosexual adolescent drug abuser: on being gay in a sad family. In E. Kaufman & P. Kaufman (Eds.), *The family therapy of alcohol and drug abusers* (pp. 105-115). New York: Gardiner Press.

Double Trouble:
Lesbians Emerging from Alcoholic Families

Barbara P. Rothberg, DSW
Deirdre M. Kidder, DC

I felt ashamed. I didn't want anyone to know. I was scared to talk about it. There wasn't anyone who could understand. I felt isolated, alone and invisible. I was afraid to get too close to anyone, fearing they would discover my secret. Sometimes I felt detached, a million miles away from all the other kids. I knew I was different and that it wouldn't go away.

Alcoholism counselors and therapists treating chemical addiction, co-dependents and adult children of alcoholics (ACOAs) will easily recognize the pain of the adult child of an alcoholic who said these words. Lesbian and gay therapists have heard similar words from their patients as they struggle with their emerging identities in a world openly hostile to them. Though the words are nearly identical, therapists who work with both these populations know that it is not as simple as understanding one population and translating the material to use with the other. There are similarities and differences between the two, and there is a "dual identity" population whose needs must be understood to effectively work with them clinically (Finnegan and McNally,1987). This paper will address the issues of lesbians who grew up in alcoholic families and the influences on their development as adolescents, young women, maturing lesbians, and their evolution in relationships.

Barbara P. Rothberg is Co-Director of the Gay and Lesbian Family Project at Ackerman Institute, NY. She is also in private practice.
Deirdre M. Kidder is a chiropractor in Brooklyn, NY.

Many young lesbians become aware of their feelings early in their adolescence, though most cannot assign a name to those feelings. They know, sometimes intuitively, that there is something different about them, that they feel something their peers don't feel. Though they may not always act on these impulses, for many these feelings become the beginning of a journey of emergence. These young women grow up gay and face a whole host of issues that are strikingly similar to the issues that many ACOAs face. The lesbian ACOAs issues are, however, a compound of all the stresses of adolescent development, dysfunctional family roots, social stigmatism and homophobia.

THE ADULT CHILD OF ALCOHOLICS

ACOAs are survivors. They have paid the costs of growing up in a home with chaos, arbitrariness, and inconsistency. They have been indoctrinated into a life of secrecy which is so powerful that even the strongest and most aware children do not escape it. The rules are unspoken, yet every child knows them. No one is to tip the delicate balance.

These children understand denial. They have learned that no one is to know, and they understand that society scorns their family's lifestyle. There is little communication within the alcoholic family. Each member suffers in silence and shame.

These children often live in fear of physical abuse, and always in fear of emotional or psychic abuse. In many alcoholic families, children are exposed to inappropriate sexual behavior by parents who traditionally have poor boundaries. Whether overtly or covertly, children in these families are in some way sexually abused. They see, hear and feel mixed messages about sexuality in general. More often than not, if there is overt sexual abuse, it is the daughter who is more vulnerable to rape, incest and molestation. No wonder that they feel unloved, abandoned and uncared for. They fear the inconsistent treatment they receive, the abuse and the mixed messages and signals they get. They cannot trust their own feelings which have so often been invalidated. They fear exposure yet suffer with the weight of their family secret. ACOAs have suffered lives of isolation and invisibility. They are veterans of falsehoods, lies, myths and fantasy. They survive alone, cast adrift from other family members by shared, yet unacknowledged family pain. Because they must keep their family secrets, these children are often unable to make more than superficial friendships. They develop the facility to shrug off the pain of disappointment in their parents, and they then translate that ability into their social networks.

In an atmosphere of instability and chaos, many of these children internalize guilt that they are in some way responsible for their parents' dysfunction. Guilt pervades their lives, and these children begin to feel that they are inadequate, unlovable, and undeserving. They experience shame (Gravitz and Bowden, 1985).

Shame is the emotional condition in which the child internalizes her "badness." Her being is devastated by the messages that she receives telling her that she is in someway inherently bad and inadequate. She is ashamed of who she is, not what she does, and nothing that she does can eradicate those deep internalized feelings. Shame is an empty feeling, a feeling of personal void, of personal worthlessness. Shame is paralyzing and self destructive and leaves little room for healthy growth. Shame is all encompassing and unavoidable in a child who grows up in an environment in which she must live in fear and with a secret (Bradshaw, 1988a; Bradshaw, 1988b).

One way or another these children grow up. All are survivors and all are scarred, some more than others. They have lived lives marked by abandonment, distrust, helplessness, chaos, abuse, loneliness, shame, and isolation.

THE EMERGING LESBIAN

As the lesbian and gay rights movement has progressed in recent years, more and more lesbians are telling their stories. As they do, it becomes clear that those who grew up knowing about their lesbianism had many of the same experiences as the children of alcoholics. They too felt the shame of secrecy, loneliness, isolation, and abandonment.

An adolescent lesbian or emerging young adult lesbian, like all young women, must perform certain developmental tasks. Major tasks are identity formation, including sexual identity, along with self individuation and integration of feelings, thoughts, morals, and learned societal mores. The integration of sexuality with the emerging personality is a major life stage and one that is actively supported and rewarded in adolescents who follow the norms. Dating, engagement and finally marriage and family are the dreams of an enculturated girl. Lesbians, however, have no rites of passage or milestones to mark their development and integration of self and sexuality. In the face of the tremendous persistence of the heterosexual model, the emerging lesbian must try to achieve a resolution between the incongruency of her feelings and the negative messages she becomes increasingly aware of.

As they are growing up, lesbians first need to become aware of their feelings of attraction to other women and to struggle with self acceptance. This task is formidable in itself, but pales compared with the task of coming out to a hostile world, risking the rejection by family, friends, and society at large.

Messages about sexuality abound for the developing girl, and many of them are mixed: the virgin, the whore, the goddess, the frigid woman, the nympho, but all are heterosexual. Messages about lesbians, however, are clear. Lesbianism is not acceptable in the social environment, including school, church, friendship groups and family. Most families strongly convey heterosexual norms, whether overtly or covertly, and present only a heterosexual model. Thus there are no models for a young woman to emulate as she experiences the development of her lesbian feelings.

THE LESBIAN ACOA

A young woman emerging as a lesbian in an alcoholic family system faces a dual set of hurdles. She knows the life and shame of being an ACOA, while she has all the stresses that all lesbians face in a society that renders them deviant and invisible. The process of identity formation of a young lesbian is inexorably linked in this case with growing up in a shame-based family system where there is already a high level of stress and an intolerance for upsetting the homeostasis. Because the basis of her home life is secretive, the young lesbian ACOA has to cope not only with her fear of self revelation, but also with her family rules of "Everything is fine," and "Don't feel, don't talk, don't reveal" (Black, 1982). She is forced to live a lie of such huge and self-negating proportions that she is bound to experience a sense of poor self esteem. This is a young woman who is caught "in the closet," not of her own making. As an ACOA, though, she believes that she is responsible for her particular dilemma. As a lesbian and an ACOA she needs to develop different coping strategies.

In the face of the unrelenting chaos of the alcoholic family, each child develops a different strategy for survival. Most commonly, ACOAs adopt roles in the family which serve to help maintain status quo. Roles may be the result of birth order, e.g., the oldest child becomes the parental or care taking child. Usually children of dysfunctional families slip into their roles intuitively, and many learn how to switch from role to role depending on the needs of the family system. (Black, 1982; Satir, 1972; Wegscheider, 1981). Because these roles provide survival not only for the family, but also for each individual who adopts them, they are often carried on through life as trusted survival techniques, particularly if they worked in the past. Often, though, childhood survival techniques become the destructive baggage of adult relationships.

The parental child is the one who takes on responsibilities in the parents' absence and exercises authority in the family. In this role, she could run the house, care for the siblings, and achieve outside the home. She can "do it" without help because she had to. But in order to achieve, she has to submerge her own needs. If she is a lesbian, she has a dilemma. She is the family role model and hero, and no hero should be gay.

Diana, the oldest of three children, presented in therapy an unresolved issue with her middle brother. She was the parental child in a family with two alcoholic parents, and her siblings all looked to her for support and guidance. As a teen, she began to struggle with her then unidentified feelings of lesbianism. Finally after years of inner turmoil, she developed a good lesbian relationship and came out to her family. Her brother who had two school aged children had assured Diana that her lesbianism "doesn't matter" but told her that he did not want the kids to know that she is gay. Because of her lesbianism, she had lost the respect she originally earned in her family of origin. She was angry and hurt, felt betrayed, and resented her invisibility. Treatment revolved around helping Diana understand that her childhood role was no longer functional in her relationship with her brother and that she needed to confront his homophobia and establish a new adult relationship with him and his kids.

The most obvious role in an alcoholic family is that of the acting out child, known as the scapegoat This is the child who overtly grabs the attention of the family by such actions as being "bad," running away from home, destroying property, abusing drugs or alcohol, and underachieving. This child takes the heat off mom and/or dad by focusing attention on herself. She suffers punishment and receives negative attention from the family in her unconscious attempt to maintain its stability. If the scapegoat is a lesbian she may flaunt her lesbianism as a way of rebelling against the family norms. If she is confused about her sexuality, the scapegoat child may choose to hide her lesbianism and act out in destructive ways. When this child develops into an adult lesbian, she will be faced with the struggle of identifying her real feelings and working them out rather than following the more familiar path of destructive and self-destructive behavior.

Yolanda came to therapy with her lover, Carmen. They had been together for three years when Yolanda admitted that she had been having an affair for the past two months. She said she was angry because Carmen spent too much time away from home and didn't care about her. It was clear that Yolanda, who had been the scapegoat child in her alcoholic family, felt abandoned and began acting out, which was a familiar destructive childhood pattern. Therapy for this couple focused on learning new ways to identify and communicate feelings rather than simply to act out without thought of consequences.

The adjuster is the escape artist of the family. No one knows what she thinks, sometimes not even she does. She lives in the fantasy land of denial. She may deny her lesbianism just as she denies her family's chaos. She may be able simultaneously to act on her lesbianism and deny it. She may, conversely, use her lesbianism as her escape from the family by forming an alliance that is unacceptable to the family and further removes her from it. Her struggle is to find a way to confront her denial and to separate from the family in a fully conscious manner. She needs to find support systems to do this.

Pam came to therapy at the age of 38. She had been in a closeted lesbian relationship for the past ten years and still worried about her sexuality. Her patterns of denial from her childhood were very powerful. She resisted using words such as gay, lesbian, or homosexual in reference to herself or her lover. She reported that she and her partner had not had sex in over a year, but that early in the relationship they had had enjoyable and frequent sex. Her only prior relationship of importance had been at the age of eighteen and had been with a woman who left Pam in order to become more involved in the gay rights movement. After entering therapy, Pam returned to her family to ''help'' her mother care for her aging alcoholic father. For Pam's growth and healing, it was imperative to help her understand her prior and current denial and come to terms with her lesbianism, increase her self esteem, and confront her internalized homophobia.

The placater is the family expert at conflict resolution. This child develops the art of negotiation and compromise in order to take care of the family needs, yet her needs remain unmet. She goes out of her way to assure all around her that everything is fine. The placater has spent her childhood taking care of everyone else's needs. Since she has been the balancing point of the family, she may fear that coming out as a lesbian may jeopardize the fragile homeostasis that she has helped create. On the other hand, she is hungry for love and longs for some stability. Her struggle is to find a way to have a healthy relationship in which her needs are realized and met instead of being compromised.

Lissa was a young woman who presented with the problem of whether or not she should come out to her mother. She had fallen madly in love with her best friend, and they were developing an intimacy that she had never before experienced. She was concerned that her mother would fall apart if she knew the nature of this relationship, and she did not want her to find out accidentally. She had considered giving up the relationship, but couldn't let go and didn't really want to. Lissa needed to know that she was not responsible for her mother and that a healthy relationship could help her heal her issues of trying to meet her mother's and others' needs rather than her own.

As the ACOA lesbian develops and matures she may find that issues of her lesbianism and of her struggles as a survivor of an alcoholic family synergize and exacerbate each other. She may be in denial about her sexual identity and this denial is comfortably similar to her and her parents' denial of the alcoholism. In a relationship, she may withdraw and suppress her disappointment, as she did so often in her family or she may attempt to control her sexual feelings and channel them into the safety of a "friendship." When feelings of intimacy emerge, the lesbian ACOA fears them. She was unloved as a child and has no experience with healthy affection. Affection is confusing to an adult who didn't receive any as a child; and when she experiences it initially as an adult, the ACOA may not know how to handle it. She may feel she doesn't deserve it, she may sexualize it, or she may become obsessive about it.

Monica entered therapy after she had finished college, where she had met Janet. Janet was a very loving, nurturing friend who was affectionate, especially to Monica. Monica misinterpreted the affectionate behavior and wanted more. She was deeply hurt that Janet didn't reciprocate. She became obsessive about Janet who began to pull away from her. She was left without a friend, feeling abandoned. She needed to learn the difference between the love and affection of a friend and a sexual relationship and that she deserved both.

LESBIANS IN COUPLES

Successful coupling depends on the development of intimacy which depends on each individual's ability to share and reveal the "true" self or the deep, emotional self. If a woman has grown up in a shame-based family system, she has often obliterated that intimate true self by years of self-abnegation and feeling worthless.

Because of her socialization as a woman, she struggles with the desire to form a deep emotional bond. The fact that her love object is another woman, however, may cause her to re-experience the panic of being found out to be the "bad," shameful child she was taught she was by her dysfunctional family.

Ideally, the formation of a couple relationship should be the result of a process of emotional bonding accompanied by a healthy dose of self individuation. This is not always the case, particularly in a couple in which one or both of the partners is an ACOA. Most of these ACOA lesbians come into early relationships loaded with their lifelong baggage of shame, fear of intimacy and low self esteem. They are unsure of themselves both as adult women and as lesbians. All ACOAs fear abandonment, but lesbians are particularly fearful in that there are no social structures or rituals, such as engagement, or marriage to mark commitment. Even "dating" is unclear: who dates whom, and is a date "a date" or is it going out with a friend?

A beginning relationship for an emerging lesbian can be fraught with anxiety producing stimuli. She may be unsure of her potential partner's sexuality and may not know how to communicate her feelings of desire without risking the loss of someone with whom she has developed a bond. Occasionally, alcohol may play a role by providing the anesthetization necessary for an unsure partner to make a sexual overture in a risky environment. Here the ACOA is the champion. She knows how to work the scenario because she has seen how alcohol functions in a system. She can drink and act as an enabler in getting her partner high enough to loosen the inhibitions generated by the encounter.

Fortunately, once developed, a relationship with another woman can provide the possibilities of growth for an ACOA lesbian by providing her with an atmosphere of nurturance, support and validation. An appropriate partner is one who can allow an ACOA to develop her sense of inner self by encouraging the giving and receiving of love in a consistent manner.

Conversely, a relationship initiated by fear, alienation and loneliness, or by the desire to escape the family of origin, can become a stumbling block to development. Often, such relationships become merged or fused. The relationship that is fused is one in which the partners begin to adopt the values, thoughts, feelings and behavior of one another, becoming intolerant of independence which threatens the relationship. Fusion is all too easy for a lesbian couple who find themselves insulated in their relationship as a result of social stigmatization. This is particularly true for a lesbian couple who lack support systems. These women essentially hide out protectively, in their relationship. The net effects of fusion are for the most part negative in that the couple tends to form an unhealthy complimentarity, a situation in which each member of the couple supports aspects of the relationship that deny individual growth, self expression, and personal satisfaction (Krestan and Bepko 1980).

Fusion is an aspect of coupling that is easy for an ACOA to slip into. She is already a master at being a chameleon to survive in her inconsistent and intolerant family of origin and knows instinctively what to do in order not to upset a relationship or, worse yet, lose it. In this milieu there is little hope for ongoing adult development.

ACOAs are known for their predilection for relationships with others who are substance abusers or with others who grew up in dysfunctional families. Two ACOA lesbians who join together without the benefit of strong loving role modeling, with disorganization as the norm, and with the scorn of those around them, are more likely than non-ACOAs to experience failure in their relationships. Without intervention many of these women may endlessly repeat these patterns.

Fortunately, there are resources now available to those who want to change. The "recovery movement" is being embraced wholeheartedly by lesbians who are committed to healthy self development.

RECOVERY IN THE LESBIAN COMMUNITY

The development of the lesbian community began in the little known and often hidden places of meeting. More likely than not these safe spaces were the darkened bars where women socialized and developed their peer groups. Relationships often began awash in alcohol and furtiveness. The community drifted into an acceptance of alcoholism as a norm. The ACOA was a perfect candidate for developing this progressive disease of the lesbian and gay life-style because her chances of becoming alcoholic are four times greater than those of her non-ACOA sisters. Her shame, and the community's early acceptance of alcohol, fueled her disease. But with the awakening of the women's movement and more important-ly with the rebellious birth of the lesbian and gay rights movement in the 1969 Stonewall riots, things began to change in the lesbian community.

As the lesbian and gay rights movement has burgeoned, more lesbians have been able to come out of the closet in which they hid in secrecy and shame. A sense of empowerment has developed, and with that have come more ways for lesbians to validate them-selves as healthy, productive members of society. As a result, lesbians have been questioning every aspect of their development in light of their liberation. Though it is true that this phenomenon is more profound in larger urban areas where there are greater resources, lesbians are pushing through the boundaries imposed on them by society wherever possible. In self analysis, many lesbians have begun to see that they have been victims of sexism and homo-phobia on a grand scale. In addition, on a personal scale, many lesbians are realizing that their development as individuals in their families of origin have added to the multiplicity of their oppression.

It is in this light that the lesbian movement has embraced the recovery movement. It is no accident that the two movements have developed in the same time frame, as there is a growing desire among the disenfranchised to validate themselves in a society that has been unaccepting and often hostile to them. A large part of the recovery process involves breaking the chains of secrecy. Just as lesbians have come out, so too have ACOAs. The ACOA move-ment has grown tremendously, with a proliferation of literature, therapy groups, and 12 step groups. Lesbians too, have developed their own canon of literature, political action groups and even re-covery groups.

Therapists are being challenged with this newly identified popu-lation of ACOA lesbians, and they need to learn to identify with its struggles as they help in the healing process. Lesbian therapists need to familiarize themselves with the experiences of ACOAs specifically and with the issues of those who survived a childhood in a dysfunctional family. Therapists and counselors who have been trained in alcohol and substance abuse issues need to learn about homosexuality and the ramifications of identifying outside the social norm.

It is the responsibility of the therapist to treat these clients in an open and genuinely accepting manner. A truly open therapist must perform a rigorous self evaluation as to her/his personal feelings about homosexuality before undertaking a therapeutic role with a lesbian. If upon an honest appraisal, a therapist detects negative feelings about homosexuality, s/he should resist establishing a relationship with that client and refer her to a more appropriate therapist.

THERAPEUTIC INTERVENTIONS

The goals of therapy for a lesbian ACOA are multifold. Each ACOA must learn about her family of origin and her role in it. It is helpful to identify the position the ACOA lesbian played in her family and how others related to her. This can be done effectively through the use of a genogram, in which the therapist asks many specific questions about each family member and how they related to one another. The lesbian ACOA needs to understand what allowed her to cope with the chaos and uncertainty she surely experienced. The coping mechanisms employed probably were similar to the ones that she still uses. Does she withdraw from conflict by removing herself? Does she attempt to make peace? Does she take over and try to control the situation? And how did/does she feel about these behaviors? She will learn that her coping strategies that developed as a child probably do not work particularly well in a healthy adult lifestyle. Making these links will be instrumental in the healing process. She must learn to recognize that the damage she experienced as a child can be healed with support and that she has the right to that support.

Lesbian ACOAs need to recognize that they are not alone, that there are lesbians all over who are in the process of recovery. The sense of isolation lesbians feel as they begin to engage in the recovery movement can be overwhelming, particularly if they are in a straight environment. These women who have less access as a result of geographic location or of insulation must be exposed to all the literature that is available to them. Bibliotherapy can be of tremendous value. Womens' bookstores have a wealth of material that lesbian ACOAs will find helpful. Therapists can refer clients to mail order catalogues for lesbian books as well as ACOA literature. National lesbian and gay hotlines and nationally based treatment centers such as the Pride Institute in Minneapolis can be utilized.

ACOA meetings are an appropriate beginning for all ACOAs. However, it is important to note that a lesbian may feel further isolated and invisible at a meeting in which she may be fearful of coming out. The therapist can be very helpful by coaching the lesbian ACOA to come out. If she can begin by making a personal contact with one or several group members and come out to them first, her coming out to the group will be easier. Lesbian ACOA meetings, if they are available, can be of particular value as they will automatically be accepting of an ACOAs lesbianism. In any case a therapist working with a lesbian ACOA client needs to be particularly aware of supporting that client through the process of recovery using the twelve step program.

A number of therapeutic stages need to be considered. One is to guide the client through the process of denial to awareness. With a lesbian client this may mean that she must confront denial of her lesbianism as well as her denial of her family of origin. This work involves asking the client many questions about her feelings toward her family and about her lesbianism. The difficulties she has experienced in both arenas may be similar and very painful. She has likely experienced feelings of rejection, shame, guilt and powerlessness. Each needs to be fully explored and understood in order to achieve greater awareness.

Following awareness there needs to be a process of acceptance. There may well be intervening steps between these stages including overcoming fear, developing self esteem, learning to reach for support, accepting help, and allowing feelings to occur in a safe environment. Accepting help and reaching for support can be accomplished through task-oriented work where the therapist develops specific goals for the client to achieve. For example, a client can be asked to reach out to a particular ACOA group member with whom she feels comfortable. Possibly just meeting together for coffee and chatting outside the group will be the goal. A further task might be to share some specific difficult information or feelings with this person. As she gains acceptance from another person in a similar situation, chances are that she will begin to feel more comfortable with herself.

Grief is probable. ACOAs and lesbian ACOAs in particular have been emotionally damaged. As they begin to feel the depth of the pain they have denied, their sense of anger and grief can be overwhelming. It is most important for the therapist to provide an empathetic ear to hear the anger and grief.

As the anger and grief begin to dissipate, the client's self esteem begins to increase. These changes come naturally, though not easily. There is often a gap between how a person feels when she has made a change and her self perception which has not yet changed. It is crucial for the therapist to enlighten the client about this new growth and help her accept and integrate a new self image. Change is painful, especially for those who are new to the process. Change means eradicating the patterns that drove the client as a child and have been triggers in her adult life. It means that the client assumes a new awareness of her patterned responses, that she can identify them and abandon what no longer serves her in favor of more healthy, productive behavior.

A stumbling block for a lesbian client is society itself. Just as she must come to a stage of realizing that her family may never change, she has the added task of recognizing that society may not change in its attitudes toward her. Though she may struggle to forgive her family and come to accept them, dealing with society's attitudes may not be as easy. Rather she may need to find safety in her interpersonal development and relationships, while simultaneously developing a coping strategy to survive continuing homophobia. Effective strategies include becoming active in the movement against homophobia, choosing to come out in her personal life, and becoming more educated about homosexuality. Retreating into the closet is not helpful as each retreat erodes self esteem.

There are scores of topics relating to the issues lesbian ACOAs face that have yet to be explored. Primary among them are the various social forces operative on lesbians of color, lesbians of different ethnic backgrounds and of differing class status. There has been little research on these issues in the ACOA literature although there must be a multiplicity of differences between various groups. A large scale study on gender differences as they affect ACOAs needs to be accomplished as well. Questions on lesbian couples in which both partners are ACOAs need to be explored, as do questions about the effects on ACOAs who grew up with two alcoholic parents. As both the lesbian/gay and ACOA movements continue to grow, so too will the understanding of the linkages between the two. Hopefully, those in the helping professions will also be better prepared to support the clients who desire change.

REFERENCES

Black, C. (1982). *It will never happen to me*. Colorado: M.A.C.
Bradshaw, J. (1988a). *Bradshaw on the family*. Florida: Health Communications.
Bradshaw, John.(1988b) *Healing The Shame That Binds You*. Florida: Health Communications.
Finnnegan, D. & McNally, E. (1988). The lonely journey: Lesbians and Gay men who are co-dependent. In *The sourcebook on lesbian/gay health care (2nd Ed)*. Shernorr, Scott Ed. Washington, D.C.: National Lesbian Gay Health Foundation.
Gravitz, H. & Bowden, J. (1985). *Recovery: A guide for adult children of alcoholics*. New York: Simon & Schuster Inc.
Krestan, J. & Bepko, C. (1980). The problem of fusion in a lesbian relationship. *Family Process*, 19, 277-289.
Satir, V. (1982). *Peoplemaking*. Palo Alto, California: Science and Behavior Books.
Wegscheider S. (1981). *Another chance: Hope and health for the alcoholic family*. Palo Alto,California: Science and Behavior Books.

BIBLIOGRAPHY

Anderson, S. & Henderson, D. (1985). Working with lesbian alcoholics. *Social Work*, 30, 518-525.
Beattie, M. (1987). *Co-dependent no more*. New York: Harper & Row, Pub., Inc.
Browning, C. (1988). Therapeutic issues and intervention strategies with young adult lesbian clients: A developmental approach. In E. Coleman (Ed.), *Integrated identity for gay men and lesbians*. New York: Harrington Park Press.

Carl, D. (1990). *Counselling same sex couples.* New York: W.W. Norton & Co., Inc.

Cermak, T.L. (1988). *A time to heal: The road to recovery for adult children of alcoholics.* New York: Avon Books.

Finnegan, D. & Cook, D. (1984). Special issues affecting the treatment of male and lesbian alcoholics. *Alcoholism Treatment Quarterly*, 1, 85-98.

Gartrell, N. (1984). Combatting homophobia in the psychotherapy of lesbians. *Women & Therapy*, 3, 13-29.

Glaus, K. (1988). Alcoholism, chemical dependency and the lesbian client. *Women & Therapy.* 8, 131-144.

McCandlish, B. (1981-2). Therapeutic issues with lesbian couples. *Journal of Homosexuality*, 7, 71-78.

Nardi, P. (1982). Alcohol treatment and the non-traditional family structure of gays and lesbians. *Journal of Alcohol and Drug Education*, 27, 83-89.

Roth, S. (1985). Psychotherapy with lesbian couples, individual issues, female socialization, and the social context. *Journal of Marital and Family Therapy*, 11, 273-286.

Swartz, V. (1984). Relational therapy with lesbian couples. In *Treating Couples.* G. Weeks (Ed.) New York: Brunner/Mazel, Inc.

Treadway, D. (1989). *Before it's too late: Working with substance abuse in the family.* New York: W.W. Norton & Co., Inc.

Whitfield, C. (1989). *Healing the child within.* Florida: Health Communications.

Woititz, J. (1983). *Adult children of alcoholics.* Florida: Health Communications.

Lesbian Recovering Alcoholics: A Qualitative Study of Identity Transformation– A Report on Research and Applications to Treatment

Emily B. McNally, PhD, CAC
Dana G. Finnegan, PhD, CAC

In 1989, Emily McNally completed the above-named dissertation. The findings from this study have important implications for *all* mental health professionals, but most particularly for professionals in the field of chemical dependency treatment. This report will describe these findings and discuss their applications to treatment.

Eight women who identified themselves as lesbian recovering alcoholics (LRA) were chosen as participants in this study. They were white, middle class, employed, women between the ages of 30 and 45, from a large urban area, and were both lesbians and recovering alcoholics for at least two years. The study itself consisted of two in-depth individual interviews an hour and a half in length and one hour and a half group interview (conducted between the two individual interviews). Symbolic interactionism and some of the stage models of alcoholic and lesbian identity transformation provided the theoretical framework.

Emily B. McNally and Dana G. Finnegan are Co-Directors of Discovery Counseling Center in Millburn, NJ and New York City. They are founders and current board members of the National Association of Lesbian and Gay Alcoholism Professionals.

A distinct five-stage developmental model of lesbian recovering alcoholic identity transformation emerged. This model describes the process by which women accept and integrate the two sub-identities of lesbian and alcoholic into the single, distinct identity of lesbian recovering alcoholic. A concept central to understanding this process is that there is a powerful dynamic interaction between sexual identity and alcoholism.

STAGES IN THE MODEL OF LESBIAN RECOVERING ALCOHOLIC (LRA) IDENTITY TRANSFORMATION

I: Beginning Stage

The women reported experiencing feeling alienated, having a sense of difference, of "dis-ease" prior to any awareness of a lesbian identity. They related their sense of difference to their earliest feelings about being a girl and traced their lesbian identity back to that time. The strategies they developed to cope with their "dis-ease" were primarily denial and unawareness and/or acting out and creating a rebellious, negative identity or "persona." All of the women said their experiences in adolescence marked the beginning of their alcoholism *and* their lesbian identity.

II: Drinking Stage

There was a powerful interaction between their drinking and their sexual identity. Drinking became the primary strategy for coping with feelings about sex and sexual identity, attraction for other women, and stigma and shame. Some drank to deny fears about sex and the possibility of lesbian feelings; some drank to be *not* lesbian; some drank to *be* lesbian. Drinking prevented the women from performing many of the tasks of identity transformation. For example, "coming out," the process of accepting and integrating one's identity as a lesbian requires planning, evaluating, and developing skills for coping with the consequences of one's actions. Drinking blunts or "disconnects" the person from these skills; while drinking some of the women came out impulsively, inappropriately. None of the women got past the Immersion phase of identity transformation (Cross, 1971)[1] meaning that they could only immerse themselves in the lesbian subculture (primarily the bars) and see themselves as separate and alienated from the rest of the world. Ultimately, the women's alcoholism took over and crowded out all other identities. Their alcoholic drinking became their primary experience and identity.

III: Recovering Alcoholic Stage

There was a dynamic interaction between recovery from their alcoholism and the transformation of their sexual identity. The women had to focus first on saving their lives by transforming their active alcoholic identities to sober ones. To do so, they had to find a way to feel safe in regard to their sexual identity. Where each woman was in the development of her lesbian identity could be assessed by employing Cross's (1971) and Cass's (1979) identity transformation models. The phase each woman was in determined the kind of help she needed to get sober. Women in the first phase of sexual identity transformation were protected by denial and therefore did not, at that point, have to reveal or deal with their sexual identity. Thus they could feel safe in mainstream AA. Women in the second phase, during which a person is the most vulnerable and ambivalent, needed acceptance of their possible lesbian identity and help in focusing on their alcoholism recovery. Women in the third phase needed support for their poorly formed, negative lesbian identity or persona and help with countering the forces of homophobia. Safety enabled the women to concentrate on transforming their alcoholic identities from negative to positive; recovery enabled them to transform their lesbian identities from negative to positive. The process of recovery is one of "de-shaming" a shame-based identity; since alcoholic is a "master identity," the

---

1. Both Cross (1971) and Cass (1979) employ the term "stage" in their models of identity transformation. Because McNally also uses the term "stage" in her dissertation, we have chosen to employ the words "phase" and "level" when discussing Cross' or Cass' models.

tools used in the process of recovery helped the women de-shame their stigmatized lesbian identity. For example, the powerful teaching and experience provided by AA of belonging to a group of people who are similar and who are proud to be who they are is enormously helpful in the coming out process.

IV: Lesbian Stage

There was a powerful *circular* interaction between the women's transformation of their alcoholic and their lesbian identities. Accepting and internalizing their alcoholic identities enabled them to explore, accept, and internalize their lesbian identities which, in turn, enabled them to continue to transform and strengthen their alcoholic identities. It became clear that there is a distinct difference between being lesbian while drinking alcoholically and when sober. Those women who came out while drinking tended to be impulsive, out of control, and often experienced dire consequences. Sober, they could actively work on transforming their identity because sobriety allows the restoration of cognitive and affective functioning necessary to this work. Sobriety also made it possible for the women to move past the unmindful, impulsive, extremist third phase of Immersion (Cross, 1971). They could, for instance, come out again in a thought-out, prepared way. Yet, even in sobriety, external and internalized homophobia was still the most difficult and painful barrier to accepting and internalizing a positive lesbian identity. Nevertheless, the women's work in sobriety enabled them to experience their lesbian identity as an integral part of their overall identity.

V: On-going Management Stage

The women were involved in an on-going process of internalizing their alcoholic and lesbian identities and integrating them into a Lesbian Recovering Alcoholic identity. They had to manage the effects of having an LRA identity–primarily those created by "alcophobia" in the lesbian culture and homophobia in the mainstream AA culture. These effects included such reactions as not feeling comfortable around lesbians who drank a lot or not feeling safe at times in "straight" AA meetings.

CLINICAL PRACTICE

A number of implications for clinical practice arise from this study. Because sexual identity and alcoholism are interrelated in such complex ways, it is important for mental health professionals to be knowledgeable in both areas. In order to provide effective and ethical alcoholism treatment to women, clinicians not only must know how to properly diagnose alcoholism, they must also be able to assess the level of a woman's sexual identity formation.

Clinician's knowledge should include learning what questions to ask, when and how to ask them, as well as how to respond to the answers. For example, just asking active alcoholics how much they drink is not enough to diagnose alcoholism. Just telling someone to attend AA meetings is often not enough. Frequently the clinician must help the person cope with her fears and stereotypes about AA.

In addition, just asking a woman to disclose her sexual orientation is not enough. She may not have a sexual identity that is developed enough for her to be able to talk about it. She may be afraid to reveal what her sexual orientation is. She may be confused and ambivalent. Or she may need help putting words to her feelings and experiences. In addition, clinicians who wait for clients to raise the subject as a "problem" may never learn important information about their sexual identity. Any clinician seeing women should be alert to this fact and to the need for taking a thorough psycho-social-sexual history. It is important to ask clients about sexual and relational behaviors, feelings, and beliefs and about any questions or conflicts they might have regarding who they are.

It is critically important to provide an atmosphere in which women can feel safe enough to talk about whatever fear, anger, or shame they might feel about their actions when they were drinking or about their possible lesbian identity. Safety is created by clinicians' dedication to identifying and modifying their own homophobia and sexism, learning all they can about alcoholism and sexual identity, and being willing to admit their limitations. In addition, safety is achieved by ensuring confidentiality and accepting and understanding the client's feelings and experiences.

It is imperative that clinicians understand just how essential safety is to women trying to recover from alcoholism. The woman in the study who was the most "out" as a lesbian described her experience during the last terrible year of her drinking. In a crisis, she went to a psychiatric ward where she reports,

> I had a psychiatrist and the first thing he asked me was what was my sexuality. When I told him I was a lesbian, he said that that was part of my disease of alcoholism and that they would help me, and I said, "I don't want to be part of this treatment program." . . . Now, a person who was in as bad shape as I was did not need to hear that. I was seeing bugs on the wall and elephants on the sidewalk. I belonged in a detox. I needed a lot of help and I didn't get it. I could have been dead. I mean everywhere I went I encountered prejudice against my lesbianism–and ignorance.

This woman–who was a lesbian feminist separatist–felt safe only with other lesbians. Fortunately, she was able to find other recovering alcoholic lesbians who helped her get sober.

This study presents a fact that clinicians need to know and understand. Safety means different things to different people. Each woman had to deal with getting sober in ways that were safe for her in relation to her particular level of lesbian identity development. The most "out" woman needed other lesbians. Some of the other women who drank to be able to *act* lesbian (to be sexual, to be social, to appear tough and invulnerable) had to go to "straight" AA meetings and get straight or bisexual sponsors because they couldn't deal with both their alcoholism and their sexual identity at the same time. The fears experienced in early recovery rendered them incapable of coping with the issues and problems of being lesbian in this homophobic society.

One of the women who drank to be *not* lesbian needed help from her counselor to just put her concerns and issues about possibly being lesbian "on the shelf" for a long time while she attended to her alcoholism recovery. It took this woman six years before she could admit to her lesbian identity. Had it not been for a compassionate and wise counselor, she might have relapsed under the stress of her own internalized homophobia. As it was, at the end of her sixth year, she went to a lesbian AA group and announced her new-found identity as a lesbian. Another woman, who drank to *be* lesbian, also needed help to put aside her issues about her lesbian identity for a long time and focus solely on her alcoholism recovery. Only after she had been sober for four years could she come out as a lesbian. One woman who was in denial of her lesbian identity needed to attend "straight" AA to get sober. Only after several years could she consider the possibility that she might be a lesbian. Obviously, safety meant very different things to these different women. Had they all been treated in the same way, a number of them would not have been able to get sober–at least at the time of such treatment.

Clearly, clinicians need knowledge and training in both alcoholism and sexual identity formation and in the complex interface between them. A number of the women reported that while they were drinking they interacted with numerous mental health professionals, many of whom did not diagnose their alcohol problems. Obviously, professionals need to know and understand the symptoms of alcoholism and how to diagnose it in women. In addition, they need to recognize that being lesbian does *not* cause alcoholism nor should it be regarded as pathology which must be treated in order for a woman to get sober. Professionals should also know how to reassure women about their sexual identity conflict while helping them focus on their alcoholism.

Another important implication of this study is the need for *all* adolescent girls to have help and support for their feelings and conflicts about who they are and who they might become. These girls need knowledgeable people who are accepting and understanding about sexual identity to talk with and to guide them in the important choices in their lives. Teenage girls also need help learning to depend on people rather than on alcohol to cope with the many difficult decisions they must make in the course of their development.

During adolescence, the women in this study did not get the kind of help and guidance they needed. After getting sober they had to struggle with many of the same issues and problems they had during adolescence. They needed help in sobriety to make choices and decisions about their careers, health concerns, and lesbian identity. Clinicians should be skilled in helping them with these and other problems related to living and managing an LRA identity.

It is important to understand the different phases of sexual identity transformation in order to be helpful to women and to make appropriate referrals. For example, when a woman is struggling with the painful external and internalized homophobia that goes with the early phases of coming out as a lesbian, a non-homophobic heterosexual or bisexual sponsor may feel safer to her. Having a lesbian sponsor would very likely feel too threatening, as would attending lesbian AA meetings. It is especially important to help women protect their alcoholism recovery while they are struggling with lesbian identity.

Depending on where clients are in developing their lesbian identity, clinicians who are working with lesbian recovering alcoholics may consider doing some or all of the following. They can encourage clients to: (1) focus on AA and their alcoholism recovery; (2) talk about their feelings and conflicts about their lesbian identity; (3) work on developing a positive view toward lesbian identity; (4) read books about lesbians and lesbian identity; (5) talk with other lesbian recovering alcoholics; (6) attend a gay/lesbian AA meeting; (7) attend a lesbian AA meeting; (8) slowly explore their lesbian sexual and affectional feelings and experiment with a lesbian relationship; (9) attend lesbian social events; (10) accept a positive lesbian identity; (11) deal with self-disclosure in and out of AA.

Nevertheless, whatever the theoretical orientation of the professional, good treatment for women who may be or are lesbian relies on non-homophobic attitudes, knowledge of sexual identity development, and the ability to care and be sensitive to the issues and needs of those struggling to recover from alcoholism while dealing with a homophobic society.

LRA's Speak to Professionals

It is only fitting to end this report with the words of the courageous women who participated in this study. By sharing their pain and struggle and triumphs, they have given us a better understanding of a process long shrouded and hidden by the stigma placed on it by a homophobic society.

In response to the question, "What would you like to say to professionals about lesbian recovering alcoholics?" the women shared their concerns. Linda says, "Well, first of all . . . they're human just like any other person. They're no different in their feelings, in their intelligence, and they should be treated equal." Others comment on the need for professionals to recognize the similarities and differences which exist between lesbian and heterosexual alcoholics. As Barbara notes,

> I think that even though we are lesbians, we still have the same relationship issues as a heterosexual couple would have in recovery. Either way, we're not that different. I guess I'm not convinced that it's as important to concentrate on the homosexuality as it is on the feelings and what's going on inside. I guess I would just hate to think that someone working with recovering lesbians would think that it's a totally different ball game. I'm not so sure it is. I think my feelings for my lover are very much the same as someone else's feelings for their husband or vice versa.

Other women talk about some of the differences they think exist and suggest that professionals need to attend to them. Betty and Helen say that society's homophobic attitudes create the major difference for lesbian recovering alcoholics. Betty states:

> We have special needs and special issues that need to be looked upon, that we're not those "sick people." There's a stigma that's attached to lesbians and gay men, you know, that this is sick. I don't feel we are sick.

Betty goes on to say that homosexuality is not a disease, but that some professionals seem to think it is. She contends that the only disease is alcoholism and that professionals should attend to that and help to normalize lesbian identity.

Helen has a similar point of view. She talks about the effects of multiple oppressions on lesbians and how lesbians deal with the "extra burden that we bear." She says,

> I think . . .the rejection of society [is] that extra burden that we bear. . . . we still are not considered . . . normal people. We're not considered to be okay. I don't care how much we deny it and how rebellious and defiant we act. It hurts us and

> it reinforces our low self-esteem and it reinforces the idea that we're different and it makes us ghettoize ourselves.

Some of the women suggest that professionals should know about other special problems and issues of lesbians created by societal homophobia. They say that society makes it necessary for lesbians to seek safe places to socialize. Traditionally those places have been bars. The women comment on how much of the social life in the lesbian community has revolved around bars and how this tends to create a risk for a higher alcoholism rate.

The women talk about how important it is for professionals to know about the high incidence of alcoholism and drug abuse in the lesbian community. Mary also wants professionals to know how the heavy drug and alcohol use in the lesbian community makes it very difficult for lesbians to get and stay sober. She contends that the community does not encourage its members to go to AA and that this causes special problems for lesbians who are trying to recover. She says,

> I believe it's very difficult for lesbians to get sober and stay sober. I've met a lot of dykes socially and on my way to and from work. I'm introduced to them all the time and they are all drinking and drugging. The community is very full of drugs and alcohol. I see these babies come in and their lovers are drinking and think they are crazy for being in AA. They're not encouraged to come into the program. I think they have special problems that way.

Mary also suggests that professionals do not understand lesbians and therefore do not help them. She gives some of the reasons why she thinks professionals are not helpful. She says,

> I feel that lesbians as a group or as a community are probably some of the most misunderstood people. I think that they don't get the help that they need, even from professionals who are supposed to help them because of cliche attitudes, their own homophobia, their lack of seeing the problems. I think that a lot of us drank because we're alcoholics, but they say

that drinking is just a symptom. If that's so, I believe that a lot of my drinking was to keep me in the closet and I think a lot of women drank to stay out of the closet. Some drank to stay in it, some drank because they didn't want to be lesbians, or "why oh why can't I be normal, let me have another drink." I've heard many people say how a professional did not help them. My own professional denied my lesbianism. She believed it was a phase.

Finally, Mary's cry from the heart to professionals working with lesbian alcoholics is, "Help them, help them, support them!"

REFERENCES

Cass, V. C. (1979). Homosexual identity formation: A theoretical model. *Journal of Homosexuality*, 4, 219-235.
Cross, W. E. (1971). Discovering the black referent: The psychology of black liberation. In V. J. Dixon & B. G. Foster (Eds.), *Beyond black or white: An alternate America* (pp. 95-110). Boston: Little, Brown and Co.
McNally, E.B. (1989). *Lesbian recovering alcoholics in Alcoholics Anonymous: A qualitative study of identity transformation.* Unpublished doctoral dissertation, New York University. (University Microfilms No. 9004305.)

BIBLIOGRAPHY

Anderson, S. C., & Henderson, D. C. (1985). Working with lesbian alcoholics. *Social Work*, 30(6), 518-525.
Breakwell, G.M. (1986). *Coping with threatened identities*. New York: Methuen.
Brown, S. (1985). *Treating the alcoholic: A developmental model of recovery.* New York: John Wiley and Sons.
Denzin, N. (1987). *The recovering alcoholic*. Newbury Park, CA: Sage Publications Inc.
Finnegan, D. G., & McNally, E. B. (1987). *Dual identities: Counseling chemically dependent gay men and lesbians.* Center City, MN: Hazelden Foundation.
Kus, R. (1988). Alcoholism and non-acceptance of gay self: The critical link. *Journal of Homosexuality*, 15(1/2), 25-41.
Rudy, D. R. (1986). *Becoming alcoholic: Alcoholics Anonymous and the reality of alcoholism.* Carbondale, IL: Southern Illinois University Press.
Sophie, J. (1985/86). A critical examination of stage theories of lesbian identity development. *Journal of Homosexuality*, 12(2), 39-51.

Dual Diagnosis Issues with Homosexual Persons

Ronald E. Hellman, MD

INTRODUCTION

The evaluation and treatment of individuals with both substance abuse and psychiatric disorder is a relatively new and rapidly evolving discipline in the field of mental health (Talbott, 1989). This paper will explore how so-called 'dual diagnosis' problems may impact on homosexual individuals, and how a homosexual orientation may affect those with dual diagnoses. A clinical approach is outlined and should give treatment providers at least some context and method for better evaluation and understanding of these issues. But, this rather specific and complex subject must ultimately await future research to provide the answers needed for more rigorous guidelines and prescriptions in this developing specialty.

THE ISSUES

Although studies of dual diagnosis problems in the homosexual population are almost nonexistent, co-occurring drug and psychiatric impairment may be significant in this group. Many investigations, for example, demonstrate higher rates of alcohol abuse in the lesbian and gay community when compared to the general population (Lewis et al., 1982; Lohrenz et al., 1978; Saghir et al., 1970 A; Saghir et al., 1970 B). Since dual diagnosis studies find higher rates of psychiatric disorder in substance abusers (and vice versa), the risk of dual diagnosis problems in homosexual individuals may be higher as well.

Ronald E. Hellman is in private practice.

105

Chemical dependency and mental illness can be a consequence of each other or occur independently in the same individual. In both circumstances, there is ultimately a global impact on the person which can be magnified when the individual is also of a homosexual orientation. Dual diagnosis homosexual individuals suffer from the combined sequelae of drug abuse, psychiatric impairment, and anti-homosexual prejudice. The signs can be remarkably similar and include demoralization, shame, denial, low self-esteem, guilt, self-hatred, suspicion and anxiety.

Feelings of inferiority because of homosexuality are compounded when psychiatric disorder and drug addiction are present. Individuals who experience the triad of stigma associated with these concerns may have little hope that they can achieve a true sense of health and well-being. For some, past treatment experiences have exacerbated this conviction because homosexuality, rather than homophobia, was considered pathological. If not addressed, these feelings may jeopardize sobriety and limit the chances for a positive psychiatric outcome.

Lesbians and gay men have unique concerns that may bring them to seek therapy. These range from a desire to explore the implications of being sexually different from others, to confrontation of traumatizing and painful experiences of denigration, hatred, and rejection because of their sexual orientation. The intrapsychic and interpersonal consequences of such experiences can increase the risk for drug problems and psychiatric impairment. But drug abuse and psychiatric dysfunction can also be quite independent of sexual orientation issues. In fact, many homosexual women and men today find their sexual orientation to be a source of strength and individual identity. As one gay man states:

> *It takes some courage to be "me" and I'm proud of that. My homosexuality gives me a particular perspective on life and its diversity. It's just part of what makes me unique.*

Individuals may, therefore, present to the clinician with varying chief complaints that should be carefully assessed without assumptions. In some dual diagnosis individuals, positive aspects of a homosexual identity can be utilized as a resource in efforts to overcome drug and psychiatric disability, while for others, a focus on sexual identity conflict will be necessary if there is to be any progress with dual diagnosis problems.

The therapist who chooses to work with these individuals must be aware of and be able to address certain general difficulties. First, dual diagnosis clients, including those that are homosexual, frequently have complex, often atypical presentations that challenge the clinician's diagnostic, empathic, and therapeutic management skills. The therapist should be aware that evaluation and treatment strategies that either ignore or over-emphasize the contribution of relevant factors in each case are unlikely to succeed.

Secondly, few therapists have had formal curricular training on gay and lesbian identity development, past and present theories of homosexuality, gay lifestyles, and the effects of homophobia and stigmatization. Nor have most therapists had rigorous supervised clinical experience in history taking, clinical assessment, and therapeutic interventions with gay men and lesbians (Hellman et al., 1989). This lack is further complicated by the relative paucity of research, clinical information and experience with dual diagnosis clients. To redress these deficiencies, therapists should read (see references for several basic texts), attend educational presentations, and seek supervision and consultation with colleagues experienced with these issues.

Thirdly, drug and psychiatric programs have been criticized for overlooking factors outside their respective disciplines. This is an important consideration with this special population, not only in relation to their dual diagnosis status, but because few such programs routinely provide an agenda that addresses the concerns of homosexual men and women. Furthermore, for the homosexual individual, mental illness and drug addiction can be barriers to acceptance within the gay community. For these reasons, an informed and supportive therapist may be the only vital resource available to these patients.

Careful, sensitive evaluation and observation will enable the therapist to determine the extent to which homosexual issues are contributing to the psychiatric and drug picture and the degree to which psychiatric and drug issues are impacting on a homosexual lifestyle. Evaluation begins with standard methods of assessment for drug use and psychiatric syndromes, since the clinician is likely to encounter individuals with presentations that run the gamut of mental distress. Review of past treatment records, discussion with significant others where possible, and performance of a physical examination and toxicology screen further establishes a reliable base of information that allows for a meaningful treatment plan.

Consultation should be generously utilized, as few therapists have the knowledge and training to fully evaluate and treat the wide breadth of issues that may be present, ranging from post-drug organic impairment to anti-homosexual religious indoctrination.

Inquiry about sexual orientation and its clinical significance, often neglected, should become an integral part of the initial assessment. The clinician will need to determine the extent to which individuals understand, distinguish and accept their drug and psychiatric disorders as well as their homosexual orientation. Is homosexuality, for example, considered to be a sin, crime, psychiatric disorder, lifestyle, or personality trait? How well-integrated or dissociated is the individual with respect to these issues? How stigmatized is the person's identity because of them? How dysfunctional is he or she because of stigmatization? How does the client view the therapist's inquiry into these topics?

Several sessions may be necessary to gather the needed information. Investigation of sexual identity in the dual diagnosis patient can initially proceed with an approach that frames the inquiry within a context that considers the impact of the social environment. Questions focused on stigmatization within such a psychosocial context may be experienced as less threatening than more intrapsychically-oriented questions that may be perceived as implying individual pathology.

In this approach, the relevant portion of the interview might be directed in the following manner: *Have you ever been shunned, criticized, rejected by others because of your drug use? . . . mental symptoms? . . . sexual preferences? What is your sexual orientation? Who are your sexual partners?* Questions are framed in gender-neutral terms to avoid any bias regarding sexual preference.

If a homosexual orientation is established, questioning may then proceed into areas that expand on the meaning and context of homosexuality for that individual: *What do you think about your ho-*

mosexuality? Be specific if necessary. *Do you think it is a sin? mental disorder? personality trait?* etc. *Are you open about it with others? With whom?* Links with psychiatric symptoms and drug use can be established here as well. Homosexuality, for example, is often considered more unacceptable than drug use and patients may report being more secretive about it. *How have drugs (or mental illness) affected your homosexual lifestyle (friendships, sexual activity, romantic involvements, etc.)? Do you think your use of drugs or mental difficulties are related to your homosexuality?*

Does your family know about your homosexuality? How did they react? Negative family attitudes about homosexuality often contribute to psychiatric morbidity and drug abuse in lesbians and gay men. *Have religious beliefs conflicted with your homosexuality? Have you ever discussed your homosexuality with a therapist before? What was the attitude in previous treatment settings?* Religion and psychiatry have traditionally been sources of negative and pathological views about homosexuality that may engender dual diagnosis problems.

Further questioning will depend on the individual's specific circumstances and may include inquiry that establishes links with academic, career, and health issues. Homosexual men, for example, are at high risk for AIDS. This stressor may contribute to psychiatric morbidity and drug abuse, on the one hand, while mental illness and intoxication can impair judgment, impulse control, and interpersonal relations so that the danger of high risk sexual activity may be greatly increased.

The clinician should establish whether homosexuality is a lifelong, stable, trait-dependent orientation, or a transient state-dependent phenomenon such as a delusion or behavior reflecting drug intoxication. Homosexuality, for example, may be a form of acting out behavior in otherwise heterosexual individuals. In those with personality disorders, for instance, homosexual behavior may represent the self-punishing indulgence of a masochist, the impulsive nurturance-seeking of a borderline, or the manipulative and dominating exploitation of a sociopath. Sexual orientation is rarely a monolithic phenomenon, and the extent of fluidity and indeterminacy should be so indicated.

Note whether homosexual acts and beliefs occur only at the time of other psychiatric and drug symptoms, or whether they are consistently present. This is sometimes difficult to determine without further corroboration and assessment that supports the initial clinical impression:

A 32 year old black male presented to a therapist in an intoxicated state saying that his neighbors were taunting him because he was homosexual. Further information was elicited from his wife, who established that there was a history of prior treatment in the clinic. Past treatment records gave a history of recurrent paranoid episodes, and his wife indicated that when not symptomatic, he was a loving father and intimate husband. His drinking began shortly after he became paranoid but resulted in an escalation of his fear of mistreatment by his neighbors. He was diagnosed with a delusional disorder, persecutory type (probable) and alcohol abuse secondary to the paranoid disorder (American Psychiatric Association, 1987). He was treated with an antipsychotic medication with resolution of his delusional beliefs. He confirmed that he had no significant homosexual interest and got along well with his neighbors. He returned to his family without further abuse of alcohol, resuming an active heterosexual life. His diagnosis was modified to eliminate "(probable)" because there was no longer uncertainty as to whether he was the victim of neighborhood homophobia and he did not express concern about his sexual orientation. This patient's homosexual focus was secondary to a brief paranoid state that resolved with medication. Not everyone that presents with a homosexual preoccupation has a sexual identity issue that needs sorting out.

Next, determine how patients feel about their sense of masculinity or femininity, since some individuals misinterpret sex role inadequacy as a sign of same-sexual orientation. Conversely, in some subcultures, dominant males who engage in homosexual activity may not label themselves as "gay," but may assent to the description of being a "man who has sex with men." Questions can be posed that ask about the patient's concept of being "a man" or "a woman" and the extent to which the patient fits this ideal role. Sex role can then be distinguished from sexual fantasy and activity. A further consideration of homosexuality and its relation to the various psychiatric diagnostic categories can be found in the article by Smith (1988).

Direct and specific questioning about psychiatric disorder, drug use, and sexual orientation is a therapeutic, as well as an evaluation strategy, because such questioning helps to overcome the secretiveness and denial that are associated with stigmatizing issues. Open-ended interviewing is generally not a sufficient method with these individuals because of the risk of collusion with this denial. In addition, asking patients how they feel about such questioning begins a process in which interpersonal issues experienced in the therapy can be shared.

Questioning about sexuality and homosexuality can be discomforting. Patients may cooperate more readily if this is acknowledged. The therapist can preface the inquiry by saying: *I would like to ask you some personal questions. I know that sometimes we feel uncomfortable talking about certain subjects, but I want to make sure that we don't miss any area that could be important in helping you to feel better.*

The clinician must assess each case individually, seeking to establish the unique extent to which drug, psychiatric, and homosexual factors contribute to the presenting problem. Establishing the longitudinal time-course of events in the patient's life is a useful technique in clarifying the relative independence or association of the various factors. The potentially complex interaction of determinants in dually diagnosed homosexual individuals warrants that the clinician avoid premature conclusions as to the relative contribution of each. When there is uncertainty as to the relevance of any factor, this should be so indicated.

A 54 year old white, lesbian female was admitted to the hospital after attempting suicide with an overdose of valium and alcohol. Her partner of 18 years reported that she had always been secretive about her homosexuality, drank heavily for many years, and for the past two months had lost a considerable amount of weight, feeling that life was hopeless.

Diagnostic possibilities in this case include a major clinical depression, adjustment disorder with depressed mood, organic affective syndrome, dysthymic disorder, and sexual disorder, not otherwise specified (discomfort with sexual orientation)(American Psychiatric Association, 1987).

Because her depressed mood, decreased appetite, and hopelessness persisted 2 weeks after detoxification, an organic affective syndrome was ruled out. A long-standing history of unhappy mood prior to her clinical depression of 2 months was reported. Because no specific stressor could be identified in the past 6 months, and her unhappiness had been present for many years, an acute adjustment disorder was ruled out. Problem drinking began at the age of 28 in response to anxiety about dating other women. Alcohol exacerbated her unhappy mood, but her drinking increased in response to this mood change. Although she blamed her homosexuality for her condition, saying 'I'm no good,' emotional neglect in childhood was felt to contribute significantly to her chronic lack of self-esteem.

She was treated with a course of antidepressant medication and individual psychotherapy. She attended a gay A.A. group twice a week, and her partner joined a local Al-anon meeting. One year later, she was free of depression and sober, but remained dysthymic.

Final diagnoses were major depression, alcohol and benzodiazepine dependence, dysthymic disorder, and sexual disorder NOS (provisional). The provisional diagnosis indicated uncertainty as to the source of her distress (sexual orientation? childhood neglect? etc.). Family therapy was recommended.

The broadest objectives of treatment are to achieve sobriety, psychiatric stabilization, and positive integration of a homosexual orientation. These goals depart significantly from historical approaches that considered a homosexual orientation to be an illness. Some patients may voice superficial acceptance of their homosexuality, but continue to believe that if only they could be "cured" of their homosexuality, they would be "normal" and would not have drug and psychiatric problems. A fundamental task of therapy with these individuals is to distinguish major psychiatric disorder and drug addiction, as primary mental illnesses, from a homosexual orientation as a natural and healthy variant of personality despite past stigmatization. The individual must, therefore, begin a process of recovery not from homosexuality, but from the consequences of anti-homosexual prejudices.

Homosexuality will sometimes appear to be an incidental finding in the dual diagnosis patient. Some of these individuals, however, may be unable to address psychiatric and drug issues that are independent of homosexual concerns, unless a trusting alliance is formed that is based on affirmation of the sexual orientation. Even a simple statement, such as "You seem fairly comfortable with your sexual orientation" may suffice. This recognition and acknowledgment helps to establish a fundamental empathic bridge between the therapist and patient that strengthens the therapeutic alliance by reducing the alienation and distrust that is experienced by the stigmatized individual. The patient comes to perceive that the therapist "understands who I am" in a supportive and uncritical way. This interpersonal validation fosters a process of positive self-assertion that is essential in long-term recovery.

An effective treatment strategy will consider specific solutions for specific problems. As examples, medication to palliate major psychiatric symptoms may be required in addition to the need for detoxification from abused drugs. Monitoring of drug use or abuse through regular toxicology screens and serum medication levels may be indicated to verify compliance with treatment or to clarify the probable cause of on-going symptoms. Same-sexual partner couple's counseling might address co-dependency issues, while family-of-origin therapy explores drug, psychiatric, and homosexual stigmatization as a barrier to the integration of the same-sex couple into family life.

Misconceptions and lack of knowledge regarding homosexuality, drug and psychiatric disorders can be corrected through formal psychoeducational groups and pertinent literature. Clinicians should also familiarize themselves with relevant local and national community resources that are now available for homosexual individuals (Vachon, 1987).

Dual diagnosis programs are currently in short supply. Comprehensive programs that actively and sensitively address the concerns of homosexual individuals are even rarer. When treatment programs do not offer a comprehensive approach that addresses the individual's drug, psychiatric and homosexual concerns, a knowledgeable and caring therapist becomes essential in coordinating and supervising the treatment.

The client, for example, may have to separately attend a psychiatric clinic, drug program and gay self-help group, and may receive conflicting messages regarding therapy at each. The extent of homophobic intolerance will vary from program to program. And some groups without a specific drug or psychiatric focus within the gay community may be intolerant of the dual diagnosis individual. In these circumstances, splitting often occurs–the individual may be open about homosexuality or drug and psychiatric problems in one situation but not others.

This state of affairs can challenge both the therapist's and patient's resolve and threaten compliance with treatment. A proficient and sensitive therapist can provide invaluable support through this process, helping the person to tolerate and see through conflicts, while reinforcing a 12-step commitment (see later).

A 24 year old effeminate, gay male I.V. drug abuser with a past history of attention-deficit hyperactivity disorder was referred to a drug halfway house program. The program director indicated that this client would qualify for admission because the psychiatric disorder had been in remission since adolescence, but informally advised against entry because of the 'rough atmosphere' in the program and concern for the welfare of this patient. The therapist was able to arrange placement in a more tolerant psychiatric residence by emphasizing that the drug use was in remission. The therapist gave a primary psychiatric diagnosis of adjustment disorder secondary to the social turmoil brought on by the history of atypical gender and cognitive behavior, and indicated that the drug use had been a significant complication of this. The patient agreed that the living arrangement would be contingent upon attendance at a local gay Narcotics Anonymous group, and the patient's NA sponsor would verify his attendance.

Dual diagnosis patients tend to feel alienated in programs that only focus on one major problem area. Homosexual patients may feel alienated in both psychiatric and drug programs. Particularly when a multi-problem/solution approach involves more than one treatment setting, the patient may be left with a sense of fragmentation. A comprehensive treatment approach, therefore, must be an affirmative and unifying experience. A concerned therapist, again, serves as the integrating force in this process. By applying a unifying concept to the treatment, the therapist helps to promote this sense of integration.

One way to do this is through the use of a 12-Step program. Utilizing a modified 12-Step approach can help bring together the entire treatment process. Here the therapist assists the client to:

1. admit to the powerlessness over drug addiction, psychiatric disorder, and homophobia that had rendered the individual's life unmanageable
2. admit to the need for outside help
3. act on this realization
4. address the personal impact of drug addiction, psychiatric disorder, and a homosexual orientation
5. learn to live true to oneself as a person recovering from psychiatric illness, drug abuse, and homophobia
6. further utilize outside help when needed to reinforce self-acceptance and forgiveness
7. acknowledge and accept personal limitations
8. acknowledge interpersonal issues that have arisen because of the psychiatric disorder, drug problem, and sexual orientation
9. act to resolve these interpersonal problems
10. affirm a lifelong commitment to recovery
11. accept guidance whenever necessary for self-improvement
12. share an awakened insight and spirit with others.

Engaging and maintaining the dual diagnosis homosexual individual in a recovery process requires a strong therapeutic alliance. This can more readily occur when both the expressed and hidden concerns of the individual are perceived to be sensitively and competently addressed. A part of this process requires that the clinician look at personal issues that may interfere with the ability to evaluate and treat these individuals. Such issues are probably common in a relatively homophobic society.

The bias for therapists can be subtle, often involving unconscious identification with negative social attitudes or outmoded professional views. Earlier in this article, for example, it was suggested that a person's homosexual identity could be utilized as a treatment resource in some individuals recovering from drug and psychiatric problems. Readers that found this suggestion to be discomforting or unorthodox may have discerned an element of negative homosexual bias within themselves.

The therapist should be able to explore both positive and negative aspects of the homosexual difference in their patients. A balanced and comfortable approach requires that therapists recognize and work through their own negative sentiments and irrational beliefs regarding homosexuality. On-going education, training, supervision, counseling, and direct experience with dual diagnosis homosexual individuals will enhance the therapist's ability to understand and relate to the special issues of this diverse population, and to address the countertransferential problems that may arise.

Dual diagnosis homosexual patients require rigorous, nonjudgmental evaluation and treatment. Solutions to their problems often require patience, creativity, and flexibility. As long as deficiencies in addressing these issues continue to exist in the traditional mental health care system, an attitude of caring on the part of the clinician may well be the most critical factor in mobilizing the forces of recovery with this diverse and challenging group. Beyond any specific knowledge and technical ability, the effective therapist must be able to reach out to troubled spirits with warm human contact and empower patients by encouraging their faith and optimism in themselves (Wheeler, 1990). Such an enlightened approach can help restore homosexual dual diagnosis individuals to a sense of pride in sanity, sobriety, and sexual identity.

REFERENCES

American Psychiatric Association. (1987). *Diagnostic and statistical manual of mental disorders* (3rd ed., rev.).Washington, D.C.

Bayer, R. (1987). *Homosexuality and american psychiatry*. New York: Basic Books.

Finnegan, D.F., & McNally, E.B. (1987). *Dual identities: Counseling chemically dependent gay men and lesbians*. Center City, Minn.: Hazelden Foundation.

Gonsiorek, J.C. (Ed.). (1985). *A Guide to psychotherapy with gay and lesbian clients.* New York: Harrington Park Press.

Hellman, R.E., Stanton, M., Lee, J., Tytun, A., & Vachon, R. (1989). Treatment of homosexual alcoholics in government-funded agencies: provider training and attitudes. *Hospital and Community Psychiatry, 40,* 1163-1168.

Hetrick, E., & Stein, T. (Eds.). (1984). *Innovations in psychotherapy with homosexuals.* Washington DC: American Psychiatric Association Press.

Isay, R.A. (1989). *Being homosexual.* New York: Farrar, Straus, Giroux.

Lewis, C.E., Saghir, M.T., & Robins, E. (1982). Drinking patterns in homosexual and heterosexual women. *Journal of Clinical Psychiatry, 43,* 277-279.

Lohrenz, L.J., Connelly, J.C., Coyne, L., & Spare, K.E. (1978). Alcohol problems in several midwestern communities. *Journal of Studies on Alcohol, 39,* 1959-1963.

Marmor, J. (Ed.). (1980). *Homosexual behavior a modern reappraisal.* New York: Basic Books.

Saghir, M.T., Robins, E., Walbran, B., & Gentry, K. (1970 A). Homosexuality III. Psychiatric disorders and disability in the male homosexual. *American Journal of Psychiatry, 126,* 1079-1086.

Saghir, M.T., Robins, E., Walbran, B., & Gentry, K. (1970 B). Homosexuality IV. Psychiatric disorders and disability in the female homosexual. *American Journal of Psychiatry, 127,* 147-154.

Smith, J. (1988). Psychopathology, homosexuality, and homophobia. In Ross, M.W. (Ed.), *The treatment of homosexuals with mental health disorders* (pp. 59-73). New York: Harrington Park Press.

Talbott, J.A. (Ed.). (1989). Special section on dual diagnosis. *Hospital and Community Psychiatry, 40,* 1019-1049.

Vachon, R. (Ed.). (1987). *National directory of facilities and services for lesbian and gay alcoholics.* Ft. Wayne, Ind.: National Association of Lesbian and Gay Alcoholism Professionals.

Wheeler, H.B. (1990). Shattuck lecture–Healing and heroism. *New England Journal of Medicine, 322,* 1540-1548.

Planning
an Experiential Weekend Workshop
for Lesbians and Gay Males
in Recovery

Michael Picucci, BS, NCAC II

This article presents the mechanics of planning an experiential weekend workshop for gays and lesbians while providing a framework for understanding the benefits of experiential process and the parameters of Stage II recovery.

My own personal experience with "experiential process" has made me a proponent of experiential therapy as it is described in this article. In November of 1978 I was 32 years old and had been in individual and group therapy for close to three years. I had participated in numerous growth and human development experiences; after all, it *was* the 70's. To my way of thinking I had been out as a homosexual for ten years and was well-adjusted. I was sober for one year. I was a very motivated person who wanted nothing more than to feel healthy and whole and to find freedom from the subtle, constant ache inside that kept compelling me to act compulsively and often self-destructively. There seemed to be one looming problem in my recovery: I could not really get in touch with my feelings. There was no question from my therapist that I dreaded more or that made me feel more inadequate than, "Michael, how do you feel about that?" I had no idea how I felt. It was as though all my

Michael Picucci is an addictions counselor/psychotherapist in New York City and facilitates several experiential workshops annually on Stage II Recovery, Gay and Lesbian Spirituality and Healing from the Wounds of Sexual Abuse for Men.
He is presently working on his PhD in Psychology at The Union Institute.

feelings were frozen or set in cement. I could tell horrendous stories about my growing up years and life traumas, but each was a shallow narrative without the slightest tinge of emotion. I knew something was missing, but I did not have a clue as to how to find it. Apparently, neither did my therapist at the time as she struggled to help me.

In October of 1978 I was contacted by a friend who said he had heard about a weekend *experience* workshop exclusively for gays and lesbians that was being held in San Francisco and he wanted me to go with him. On the first morning of the workshop the facilitator gave a talk on his experiences of growing up gay, and we did some small and large group structured sharing about our own growing up gay experiences. By 11:30 that morning something started to happen inside me. It was a bit scary, yet exhilarating and exciting at the same time. My feelings were coming alive. Hearing other men and women (and a very respect-worthy facilitator) share their terrible stories of isolation, humiliation and pain from growing up gay and different and hearing the specifics that mirrored my own long forgotten sorrows made each and every person in that room appear immediately courageous and even heroic to me. Being able to see and feel other gays and lesbians as courageous and heroic allowed me to see and feel that in myself. For the first time in as long as I could remember I felt worthy and courageous enough to see and acknowledge my years of pain, self-loathing and repression around my sexual identity. I saw my own denial and cover-up. I could immediately see the healing that needed to be done. I sensed there was a long road ahead, but I finally felt a strong sense of clarity and empowerment.

By unfreezing those repressed feelings, I was energized and felt a spiritual connection to my gay and lesbian brothers and sisters. For the first time, I *felt* that we were travelers sharing a unique and privileged journey together. I am pleased to report that today, some fourteen years later, I continue on this path and that the connections on both the spiritual and interpersonal levels have grown deeper and broader. Waking up and touching this core area of my life was my entree into my personal world of feelings and healing that has brought me illumination and a better understanding of many other facets of my life. Since that first weekend in San Francisco, I have been an advocate and student of experiential therapy as an augmentation of other more traditional modalities. My experience with it over the years has convinced me that although experiential therapy may serve as an introduction to psychotherapy for some, it is most productive when used in conjunction with ongoing psychotherapy. For many of the workshops I facilitate, being anchored in therapy is a prerequisite.

WHAT IS EXPERIENTIAL THERAPY?

Experiential Therapy blends together many therapies and incorporates group dynamic techniques through the use of sharing, role-playing, psychodrama, sculpturing, visualization, touching/sensitivity exercises and mirroring to achieve a desired result. It is an excellent tool for progressing a person from Stage I recovery, which is focused on getting the addiction in check, to Stage II recovery, which "is the rebuilding of the life that was saved in Stage I" (Larsen, 1985). Basically, the goal of Experiential Therapy "is to free a person from the unresolved emotions around relationships so that he/she is more free to live in the present" (Cruse, 1990). Proponents believe that this kind of therapy "is the most effective and useful tool in the healing of old pain and the developing of new possibilities" (Cruse, & Bougher, 1990). It enables participants to bring the discoveries and insights from talk-therapy and self-help groups to a feeling, experiential and even spiritual level. Typical statements received from participants, often weeks later by mail, are "It was the kind of experience I have been looking for all my life . . . It touched all of the fundamentals of life; it opened the door to think about them–and gave me a perspective that I shall never forget . . . I feel that what we experienced should be packaged and be made mandatory for each gay and lesbian in the world to experience" (This participant was in therapy and recovery for more than five years). One therapist in recovery who participated in a weekend wrote "I feel changed . . . and I feel privileged for the opportunity to engage in that process with such exceptional people." This colleague has since become a weekend facilitator.

WHAT IS STAGE II RECOVERY?

A person realizes in Stage II that emotional damage and limitations preceded their addictive behavior. These must be dealt with in order to move on to a more emotionally connected existence. In the clarity of sobriety an individual may realize that he or she tends to act out in other self-destructive ways such as involvement with abusive or emotionally unavailable people, financially disastrous behavior, sexual compulsivity, etc. This is also a time when low self worth may become apparent, manifesting in isolation and/or depression. Close friendships or a loving, sexual relationship with a partner are particularly difficult until these issues are resolved. In this stage, one re-experiences grieving and begins to let go of original pains and hurts. This is what John Bradshaw (1988) calls the "uncovery stage" where one begins to discover an inner self or "child." As a person learns to extend compassion and understanding to his/her neglected inner child, a much richer experience of self-love and self-assertion is attained. If one does this work and learns the value of affirming messages, the unconscious gets reprogrammed with supportive images and voices that are in tune with a thoughtful, adult, sober mind.

IMPORTANT CONSIDERATIONS ABOUT INTERNALIZED HOMOPHOBIA

For lesbians and gay men there is necessary deep work around internalized homophobia that can only be done in an extraordinary safe environment. Internalized homophobia is the deep self-loathing and self-hatred that comes from growing up in a society where homophobia is the norm. "Homophobia is an intense, irrational fear and dread of homosexuality and homosexuals" (Finnegan & McNally, 1987). Many lesbians and gays are in denial about the effects of these deep feelings of low self worth, which, left untreated, result in self-sabotaging behavior. For many, the denial was an important survival tool enabling one to cover up and build a life over such a damaged self image. To allow these feelings to surface, participants must feel secure in the knowledge that there will be no negative judgement and that understanding will prevail. Thus, all the participants, facilitators included, need to be exclusively gay or lesbian. Even one non-gay person in the room significantly changes the experiential environment in that the participants will project their own homophobia onto the non-gay person and then have it mirrored back as that person's judgments, thus inhibiting the work. Interestingly, bisexual participants tend to fit in and even complement the experience. This is because they also suffer from homophobia and other complex stigmatization around their sexual identity. In therapeutic settings, bisexuals tend to embrace the sensitivity available to them in the gay and lesbian communities and the safe tone that prevails in the workshop supports all the complexity and struggle.

ELEMENTS OF THE WEEKEND WORKSHOP

The purposes of the experiential weekend are to: (1) create an environment that is dramatically safer than everyday life, enabling deeper self discovery; (2) experience feelings of self respect and self-esteem; (3) experience a sense of spirituality, love and connectedness with the human family and in particular gay and lesbian people in recovery; (4) get in touch with and come to a new understanding of the inner child, the unconscious, and the damage and confusion that lie within; (5) begin or continue a healing process specific to these early hurts and mixed messages; (6) be affirmed for work already done and the continued struggle to empower one's self; (7) get away from the daily grind and have fun in a different setting with an opportunity to meet new friends.

The name of the weekend is important. *"Gay & Lesbian Spirituality Weekend"* is chosen for three reasons: (1) as a healing and political statement, the words gay/lesbian and spirituality are positively connected; (2) this work of uncovery, sharing and healing is the core of personalized spirituality; and (3) in an experiential weekend of this nature the spirituality is felt in the powerful connections people make with the other participants and themselves. This is a demanding, intense experience and is best done with a co-facilitator.

The facilitators need the following attributes for this weekend to run smoothly: sense of timing, experiential group experience, self confidence, ability to work and plan with a colleague and to be flexible, and a willingness to self-disclose.

FRIDAY EVENING: SETTING THE STAGE (3 HOURS)

The facilitators must create the context for the workshop by getting the entire group aligned with a common purpose and providing guidelines for safety and commitment. First the facilitators introduce themselves and briefly describe what an experiential weekend is including its purposes. The participants are informed that their job is to follow instructions from moment to moment. Everything has been planned for them, and they don't have to worry about anything. It should be explained that there is a rhythm to the way the workshop will progress and they are being asked to tune into it as best they can.

To prepare for a warm-up exercise the participants break up into smaller groups of 8-10 people each (asking them to pick a group in which they do not have a close friend or intimate). While it is not detrimental to share the workshop with a friend or life companion, the small group work is best done with strangers.

Warm-up exercise: With the group in small circles the facilitator advises them to listen carefully to the instructions for the first group process. They are instructed that they will go around the circle four times, fairly rapidly, and share their response to the following questions; 1st time around, *Name and what I hope to get out of the weekend workshop.* 2nd time, *What I like about myself.* 3rd time, *What I like to do in the world.* 4th time, *What I like about my sexuality and sexual life-style.* It is helpful to put these questions on a blackboard to be referred to throughout the exercise because this exercise sets the tone for the entire weekend experience. Facilitators can anticipate that most participants will respond with questions and confusion. Instructions are given to "do the best you can in each instance." The facilitators remind the participants that this is a very personal experience. There can be no wrong answers; the whole idea is that this is an opportunity to share and discover whatever comes to mind and heart when the instructions are given. No two people are likely to have the same experience.

At the completion of the exercise a volunteer from each group shares in the larger group what the exercise was like for them. A share by one young man is an example of how this simple exercise shifted a shame-based experience for many into a positive one. He said that the thing he most likes about being gay was that when he saw a person he perceived to be gay he would catch eyes with them and feel energized, that in the seconds of that glance there was an acknowledgment of the secret world and painful history they shared. His experience always made him less lonely and part of something unique and special. This was a totally different reading than the shame-laden sexual seduction experience others had with the same kind of incident.

From this first exercise, participants can learn experientially that the weekend will be safe, instructions will be clear, and that they can go as deeply into the work as appropriate for them. This is the beginning of an interactive trance-like state that is required for successful experiential work: "trance unfolds from an experiential, interpersonal encounter in which therapist aligns with client, thereby enabling both parties to become increasingly receptive to each other" (Gilligan, 1987).

Once participants are engaged in the process, they can turn their attention to the necessary and sometimes tedious hour of setting down guidelines for the weekend. Each guideline is given a rationale so that they do not appear arbitrary. *Sample guidelines are as follows:*

1. *Attend all segments and arrive on time.* This is important because each person should feel that his/her contributions are listened to and valuable. This allows for trust to develop that the participants will be there for one another throughout the process. This helps to avoid the feelings of mistrust that were learned when important people were absent in one's past.

2. *Be open to gentle confrontation by the facilitators.* Since many participants' only group experience is 12-step meetings where there is no leader and no direct response, they need to know that this is different. It is perfectly appropriate to share upsetting feelings that may be provoked by another participant or the facilitator.

It is not appropriate to attack another participant or the facilitator with those feelings.

3. *Honor 2 minute time limits for sharing.* This rule insures that everyone stays specific to the experiential work and feelings at hand. The two minute limit is ample time to share.

4. *Surrender to the instructions and note feelings and images that come to mind.* Acknowledging that we live in a busy, outer directed world, this guideline reminds us that for this workshop we want to direct our attention inward. Also the concept of willing surrender helps each participant to ease the emotional and psychological constructs used to control our everyday feelings and thoughts in a world less safe than the workshop.

5. *Be willing to sit through any feelings of anger or boredom that might come up.* For many anger and boredom are masks for more complex and frightening feelings that lurk beneath the surface. This guideline self-empowers participants to expand their range of feelings, often enabling a breakthrough in self-realization. It is explained that participants may be uncomfortable sitting with feelings until their next appropriate sharing opportunity. For many this will be a new experience. This guideline addresses distracting behavior such as opening the window, rearranging the furniture, smoking, etc.

6. *Not interrupt another's sharing or experience.* The ''no interrupt'' guideline insures that people stay with their own process and do not interfere with others' processes. This rule means not interrupting a person speaking or any participant in the group who may visibly be experiencing intense emotion. It is explained that motivation to interrupt often comes from one's own anxiety and that each person needs to feel and work through his/her own anxiety.

7. *Bring any problems or complaints to the facilitators.* Since many people look to outer problems when they begin to become anxious or bored, this is a control over distracting themselves or others with complaints. It also assures that the facilitators are there to help each participant get his/her needs met.

8. *Agree to keep all sharing heard over the weekend absolutely confidential.* This provides the safety for people to be willing to share and process at deeper levels.

9. *No smoking or eating during sessions.* This helps to avoid additional barriers to inner feelings and makes for a more purposeful environment. Ample breaks are given for meals, snacks and smoking.

After questions about the guidelines are answered and everyone agrees they can accept them, people are asked to get up from their seats and walk around the room and shake hands with the other participants to symbolically seal these agreements and commit to the entire process. This is followed by a ten minute break.

After the break facilitators initiate a discussion on homophobia by sharing their own personal experiences with growing up gay, the coming out process and early hurts and mixed messages of homophobia. The facilitators have a responsibility to be as sincere, emotional and impactful as possible. This is the first time the emotional level of the group is being deepened. To make the point that everyone is affected by homophobia there is a call for a show of hands of those who believe they are not homophobic. The facilitators then present the supposition that all people are homophobic and that some gays and lesbians are in denial about their own internalized homophobia. Those who still believe that they have no internalized homophobia are asked to suspend that belief for the purposes of the workshop.

This discussion is a lead into the visualization exercise, *Uncovering Internalized Homophobia.* It is important to explain what guided meditation is to those who do not understand. Then the facilitators start with a basic relaxation process after which they read a carefully worded meditation such as this one. Improvisation is not recommended.

> Now in a relaxed state I am going to ask you to exercise your imagination.
> *(Pause)*
> Imagine that a movie has been made of your life, all of it.
> *(Pause)*
> Now that it is available on videotape you can take it home and watch it on your own VCR, at your leisure. You can go fast forward, you can reverse the action and go backwards or you can stop the action anywhere you want. You can stop it or

slow it down to reminisce, savor the experience or get in touch with the feelings.

(Pause)

Now that you've go it in the VCR and you know what you can do with it, I want you to begin to scan it in reverse so that you can slowly watch your own life going backwards before your eyes.

Run it back slowly, back through your recent years, into your thirties, through your twenties, through your teens, through puberty and then back into the earliest years. See if you can find the image of the first time you felt you were or might be sexually different. And remember that you can stop the action anytime you want and then start again when you want. Recall the specific incidents and the feelings attached to them.

(Pause)

Take your time.

(Pause)

See if you can locate the first time your peers realized or alluded to the fact that you were different sexually. What are the specific images and how did you feel?

(Pause)

Can you get in touch with how these feelings contributed in any way to your feelings about your sexual identity?

(Pause)

Scan forward now to the first time you were in love or had a crush. See the images. How did it feel?

Take a few seconds to remember.

(Pause)

Now, having seen, sensed and recalled some of your early experiences that shaped your feelings about yourself, it's time to turn the movie off for a little while.

Before you open your eyes and come back into the room, take another minute and examine how you are feeling about your identity as a lesbian, gay man or bisexual person tonight, right here in this room.

Take a minute.

(Pause)

Open your eyes when you're ready.

Participants are asked to reconvene in the smaller groups in order to share the experience of the meditation in the two minute allotments. At this time, it is established that each group will have a rotating, volunteer time keeper who uses a watch with a second hand and informs the person sharing when they have 15 seconds left. Because time keeping will provide necessary structure throughout the weekend, it is important to establish it clearly at this point. The whole group is given a minute to practice saying "15 seconds" and "time" out loud. As in the first small group exercise, upon completing the circle of sharing, people are asked to gather in the one large group to listen to representative shares from each group. Participants are learning the weekend rhythm of small group work followed by large group interaction.

By the end of the evening, participants are more aware of the personal impact of internalized homophobia. The facilitators purposely do not put closure on the experience, leaving the participants open and charged for the work on Saturday morning. Reference is made to the importance of tomorrow's topics to create a context of interest, momentum building and enthusiasm for the next day's activities.

SATURDAY MORNING SESSION (3 HOURS)

The morning session begins with allowing several people to share with the entire group what the evening was like and where they are at now. This will elicit a range of feelings from elation to anxiety to anger and frustration. The job of the facilitators is to encourage the continued expression of all feelings and not to address any of them individually. It is important that the facilitators not take personally someone's upset and simply ask people to stay with their feelings as they evolve and change during the weekend.

This session is centered on an explanation and exploration of the recovery process using John Bradshaw's model of recovery (1988). An enlarged copy of the model is put up on the board and participants are given copies as well. Participants are reassured when they see that there really is a charted course of recovery and that they can find themselves on it. Stage I is discussed in detail. The facilitators validate that participants have successfully accomplished Stage I and need to credit themselves. Those participants who are in their first year are acknowledged for their accomplishments in Stage I. The completion of Stage I is symbolically sealed with playing of Barry Manilow's "I Made It Through The Rain." Prior to the playing of the song, participants are instructed to close their eyes, take some deep relaxing breaths, and listen to the words. It is important to explain that the music has been chosen specifically for those words. Participants are encouraged to suspend criticism of the selection. This is apt to be a very moving experience with crying for some. Throughout the weekend it is important to have a supply of tissues and to generously dispense them to anyone who is in need.

At this point it is important for the facilitators to be in touch with the group's needs. If the level of emotion and emoting is intense, a cycle of small group sharing is indicated. On the other hand, if the group intensity is low facilitators proceed with the next planned discussion. If the facilitators miss the cues and move prematurely to the next discussion, it is important for them to demonstrate that they heard the group's feedback and are responsive. In this instance that would mean going back to a fuller discussion of the music. Such responses are particularly crucial for gays and lesbians who are not accustomed to having an authority figure respond to their expressed needs. The facilitators must be self assured enough to acknowledge that they missed the group's rhythm.

After this, the facilitators discuss Stages II and III of the model, focusing primarily on stage II uncovery issues. Following this discussion the concept of the hug break is introduced. For those who are comfortable with it, this is a time for non-sexual physical contact. It is this author's experience that the physical contact heals the pain of that moment and empowers people to be refreshed and ready to go deeper in their process. Participants are told that "hug breaks" are a tool anyone can call upon during the remainder of the weekend. The facilitators provide the guidelines to insure that individual boundaries are respected and that the physical contact ranges from a handshake to a hearty hug.

The center of Stage II, "Finding the Inner Child," is the focus after the break. Discussion is stimulated by asking, "How many people have difficulty with the inner child concept or think it's just a bunch of psycho-babble?'' First people respond; then, those having success with the inner child concept are asked to share. The facilitators take the discussion to a deeper level by self disclosing. They model the usefulness of conceptualizing "the inner child" as a way to re-access early unconscious formations, i.e., a facilitator may share his awareness of the impact of being called a sissy at five and six years old contributed to his adult fear of being successful. This tool allows healing, which "is to enter with compassion and awareness that which you have pulled back from in judgement and fear and anger'' (Levine, 1988). This inner child work can range from conceptualizing one's childhood self for the first time to developing the compassion and understanding that leads to the spiritual connection necessary for Stage III. This spiritual connection is the experience of self-love.

A few volunteers having the most difficulty are asked to participate. Working with these people in the large group makes this process tangible. They are asked to recall an incident from childhood and describe it as graphically as possible. The facilitator asks questions like "What room was it in? Who else was there? What was the color of the walls? Was there a smell that you can recall? How were you feeling? What did you do after the incident?'' The participants are taking the time to give life to a moment in their childhood by focusing on its details. The intensity of questions and everyone's attention puts them back into that experience as that child while they remain an adult. This is often the first active awareness of a relationship between the adult self and the child/unconscious. For the healing of internalized homophobia this relationship is crucially important. It allows for the reeducation of that child that though homosexuality may be different and even special, it is not bad and one need not feel ashamed for their affectionate preference and natural desires.

This work is now punctuated by a musical meditation which for many will be their first experience of physical tenderness towards self. Participants are instructed to cross their arms and place their hands on their own opposite shoulders (right hand to left shoulder, etc.) and gently rock themselves as if they were holding and rocking a child who is speaking to them through the song, "I Want To

Live" by John Denver. This musical meditation is followed by small group sharing. The facilitators make the transition to the lunch break (approximately an hour and a half) by stating that it is usual for participants to feel overwhelmed at this point and "That's OK." They assure the group with a touch of humor that the afternoon will be an upbeat discussion of sex.

SATURDAY AFTERNOON SESSION (2 1/2 HOURS)

This session begins with a discussion of the words "intimacy," "sensuality," and "sex." Initially people are very confused and lump the three words together. When the confusion is well established, the facilitators put the words up on the board in the order of intimacy first, sensuality second and sex third. Then the work of defining them as three distinct entities begins. The order is important because it provides the groundwork for a progression of experiences to follow. Each concept is defined by group members calling out words they associated with it. These associations are written under the concept being defined, creating three clear, distinct definitions.

These definitions, placed visually in front of the group, are the spring board for the next exercise. The group is asked which direction they take in attempting to have their needs met, i.e., do they meet someone and attempt to get intimate first or do they go right for sexual pleasure and look to possibly get intimate later? A facilitator dramatically walks in front of the board talking his/her way through a dating experience from both directions, first starting with intimacy moving toward sex, then in reverse. Individuals are asked to raise their hands when they identify the point of their discomfort. It should be noted that this work includes people in long term relationships. The commonality is that everyone is stuck somewhere in the process of combining intimacy and sex over time. The facilitator introduces the concept of healing the "spiritual-sexual split" as a way out of this dilemma. The split is explained as the early internalization of ideas that god, love and family are good and sex is dirty, bad and unspeakable. With such a concept how could one bond in love and bring shame-based sex into the relationship? A 15 minute break follows. By this stage in the weekend people usually initiate hug breaks if that is what they need or want.

When the group reconvenes, one volunteer is recruited. This is a person who has been participating at a high level and is approached during the break to see if he or she would be willing to participate in a psychodrama and sculpting experiential exercise. The exercise illustrates how we receive messages about sex in the developing years and the effects on sex, intimacy, spirituality, goodness and god. This exercise shifts participants from the general intellectual discussion before the break to the feeling of specific personal experiences.

The group forms a large circle with the volunteer standing in the middle. Materials required for this exercise are large placards or pieces of paper, 12″ × 14″ or larger, and several felt tip markers. Two additional volunteers are needed to put words on the placards. The person in the center is asked to look back in his/her early history and share with the group a message he/she received from the world or his/her family about sex. The person may say something like "sex is disgusting." One of the writers is asked to put that on a placard in large letters. The person in the middle selects someone else from the group to represent that message, and that person holds the placard facing the person in the middle. This is the start of a smaller circle around the person. A second message is solicited. It may be, "All queers should be castrated." This second message is put on a placard and another person is selected to represent the message and join the inner circle. This is continued until there are at least eight messages in the inner circle. The placard holders are asked to turn the placards toward themselves and read them loudly clockwise at the person in the center. They are instructed to keep reading their messages louder and faster until the facilitators stop them. This should continue for at least a minute until it is evident that there is great discomfort in the room. This could happen either first with the person in the center or other group members. At a workshop for men who were sexual abuse survivors the reaction to this exercise was so powerful that when the man in the middle started to cry all nine men in the circle around him had uncontrollable tears rolling down their faces. Several had complained that they could not cry and had not since childhood. It was a profound experience for the entire group, as everyone was identifying with the process.

To illustrate how these messages prevent the coexistence of intimacy and sex the second part of the exercise is an opportunity to ritualize letting go of these messages. The person in the middle selects a group member to role-play his/her lover. The "lover" stands 12 feet away from the inner circle. The "lover's" job is to report throughout the exercise how much emotional access he/she feels he/she has to the partner in the center. The inner circle is asked to go around one more time reading their messages. It becomes crystal clear how the messages make it impossible to have sexual intimacy. The next step is to coach the center person to identify from whom they received each message. Then they are asked to assign other group members to represent each of these persons from the past. All these historical persons are placed together in a location in the room but outside the inner circle. The person in the center reads a message, recognizes that it never really was his/hers and returns it to the person who originally stated it. The center person is asked to change each message to a positive one (e.g., sex is good and healthy). After each message is given back, the "lover" is asked how she/he is feeling with regard to closeness. By the end of the exercise the "lovers" usually report feeling very close with all obstacles (or walls of shame) gone. And the whole room tends to feel the same way. This process educates and empowers the participants to recognize and deal with these messages. A hug break is an excellent way to end this afternoon section. Free time and dinner is approximately three to four hours.

SATURDAY EVENING SESSION (3 HOURS)

There are three options for Saturday evening. If the facilitators are not too fatigued, they can use the following exercises to continue in the workshop format. The other alternatives are either a 12-step meeting or a planned social activity. If the option chosen is the exercises, each participant is given a yellow pad and the following instructions: each is to write two or three letters in the next hour of quiet time. These letters, written in a stream-of-consciousness approach, tend to bring forth a great deal of emotion and clarity consolidating what has been learned to this point in the workshop. It is suggested that a letter be written to each parent or other important persons and to their child within. They are instructed to use this as an opportunity to say what needs to be said to these important persons. This is to be done in the room privately and without talking. They are advised to write quickly and freely from their emotions. There is no need to be concerned about penmanship, spelling or grammar and no one else will read these letters. The facilitators begin the hour of silence with a short meditation and prayer, which sets the dramatic, serious tone required.

This prayer is to our God, however each of us may define that force in our lives. Perhaps the term used by our Indian brothers and sisters might be most appropriate; simply "The Great Spirit." Whatever our experiences or perceptions or differences may be, we can agree that there is a spiritual force in our lives today, to whatever extent we are able to open ourselves to it.

Tonight we are gathered together in this room and each of us, in our own way, invites the Great Spirit to join us and bring grace and dignity to our experience tonight, and for tonight this room becomes a sacred place. We ask, again each in our own way, that we be able to give enough love and support to ourselves and each other so that all our negative judgements begin to evaporate, that all fear dissipates, that we may all share in a sense of love, forgiveness, and caring. We want to fortify our courage so that we can give permission for everyone in the room, including and especially ourselves, to touch and to explore the most vulnerable and fragile parts of ourselves. We want, dear spirit, to lay some burdens down. We know we are a brave and strong people. We have had to be. We claim our strength and courage now. For we know, even as we sit here now, that on the other side of these burdens and unsaid words, feelings, and thoughts-on the other side of all this-is love, which is our essence. We know this instinctively.

We feel a sense of spiritual guidance as we complete some of our communications tonight and we welcome our spiritual essence or our child within to come to the fore so that we may experience more of the beauty, love and wonder that is rightfully ours and has been in various levels of concealment for far too long.

In closing this prayer we thank you Great Spirit for leading us to sobriety, to each other and to this evening. Thank you.

There is a 15 minute break at the close of the hour's writing.

Each person is asked to pick a partner and these two people read their letters to each other. They are encouraged to read the entire letters. However, individuals may choose not to share sensitive issues in portions of the letters. This permission protects anyone who does not feel safe to share the entire letter. The partners are designated A and B. A shares all three letters first. The person who is listening is instructed to quietly "be there" and hear their partner's words and feelings, without interruptions or discussion. When A is finished, B reads all three letters. With gays and lesbians the letters will often include coming out to parents or other important people. Many people have later mailed these letters or revisions of them. Most participants experience a profound sense of cleansing and liberation when this exercise is undertaken at this time in the weekend.

After a short break, the A and B pairs reconvene and participate together in a physical healing exercise. It is an experience of being supported in as comfortable a physical position as possible. Partner B sits back into partner A's seated cradle and as the music plays B will relax against A and A will hold and rock B, giving nonsexual healing touch and energy throughout the music. The facilitators demonstrate this. When the music is over A and B will switch places and the song is repeated. One of the songs used is "Welcome to This World" by Robbie Gass. This exercise is the beginning of closure for the weekend. From this point on all exercises and presentations are fun in nature as their purpose is to prepare people for transition from intense emotional work to everyday life.

Participants are instructed to sit in a circle on the floor. In keeping with the work on closure one of the facilitators then begins the last exercise of the evening by sharing a "moment of wonder" from his/her childhood. Each person gets a turn. It is this author's experience that participants do come up with a moment of wonder and the composite experience of all of the individual joys create a shared moment of magic in the room. Because of the unique openness and power in the room, the stories that people tell come alive and incredible laughter and healing are also present. After all have shared, the evening ends with a "hug break."

SUNDAY MORNING SESSION (3 HOURS)

This session starts with open sharing by participants, followed by an opportunity for the facilitators to address any issues brought to them by individuals. Next, a brief review of the weekend is given. Lastly, suggestions are made on how to bring the empowerment learned in the weekend into daily life and how to foster that sense of empowerment. A ten minute break follows.

During the break, chairs are arranged in the circle equal to one half of the participants. Half sit in the chairs while the other half stand behind the chairs. Those standing are instructed to think of something they always wanted to hear as a child, something affirming. Those seated are asked to close their eyes and relax. Those standing will gently touch the shoulders of the person sitting in front of them and whisper the affirmation in their ear. The facilitators motion that those standing move to the next seated person to deliver the affirmation anew. It is important to allow sufficient time for the message to be received and digested. When each person standing has whispered to each person sitting, the positions are reversed and process repeated. At this point in the workshop there is an unparalleled sense of safety and trust that most participants feel. These affirmations, combined with gentle touch, tend to affect people in a deeply healing way. This exercise is followed by a ten minute break.

Participants put final closure on their experience by using two minutes to say anything they need to say or share so that they can leave the workshop feeling complete with their communications. This is done at a podium (if available) in front of the group. The sharing is often quite charged and heartfelt, and sometimes people choose to use this time to read a favorite piece of poetry or sing a song. After everyone has had a turn, words to a song are distributed and everyone sings along to the recording. An example of a closing song is "I Can See Clearly Now" which has been recorded by several artists. The closing luncheon completes the weekend.

SUMMARY

Gay men and lesbians in Stage II recovery can realize profound curative benefits from this experiential weekend workshop. In their developmental years, gays and lesbians rarely had any support with their fragile and evolving sexual identity and difference. The design of this workshop uniquely creates this opportunity while modeling the concept of self-parenting to heal and care for one's own wounded inner child. To go back to one's developmental years using supportive therapeutic technique and group dynamics touches and begins to heal unconscious hurts and limitations. The result for many is a new sense of self respect as a gay, lesbian or bisexual person who is better prepared to meet the world on its terms, as well as their own. Often participants use this newfound sense of empowerment to make significant contributions in their communities. For some it is the beginning of a new, deeper belief that they can really attain a fulfilling, sexual, and loving relationship with a same sex partner.

In addition to healing the homophobic-related damage, it is important to note that many other issues are processed, particularly repressed feelings of rage pertaining to abuse and neglect, love that has been long forgotten, and grief. The last being significantly important with the profound loss due to AIDS that the entire community has suffered in recent years. Finally, these words written by a recent participant help to sum up the experience: "It was the most positive, rewarding experience in my 13 years of sobriety. I feel connected to the world and others in a way I never have before."

REFERENCES

Bradshaw, J. (1988). *Healing the shame that binds you.* Deerfield Florida: Health Communications.

Cruse, S.W., Cruse, J.R., & Bougher, G. (1990). *Experiential therapy for co-dependency.* Palo Alto, California: Science and Behavior Books, Inc.

Finnegan, D. & McNally, E. (1987). *Dual identities: counseling chemically dependent gay men and lesbians.* Center City. MN: Hazelden.

Gilligan, S.G. (1987). *Therapeutic trances.* New York: Brunner/Mazel, Inc.

Larsen, E. (1985). *Stage II Recovery.* New York: Harper & Row Pub., Inc.

Levine, S. & Levine, O., (1989). Living your dying. *Common Boundaries.* July/August issue.

Application of Family Therapy Concepts in the Treatment of Lesbians and Gay Men

Dava L. Weinstein, MSW

INTRODUCTION

Lesbians and gay men come from biological/blood related and adoptive families. Just as with heterosexuals, their interactive experiences with parents, siblings, grandparents, aunts and uncles, cousins and others color their life view. This article will focus on clinical interventions made possible by collecting information of a three generational nature. This is particularly important since clinicians frequently view lesbians and gay men out of the context of their biological/blood or adoptive families. Although the focus is on problems of active addiction and recovery, the concepts are applicable in the treatment of any presenting problem. The family therapy field concepts to be discussed here include clinical assessment and interventions based in a three generational context (Carter & McGoldrick, 1989), identifying organizing family themes, reframing, and the strategic technique of restraining any move towards change. The client can be an individual, couple, or family. The primary vehicle for achieving this in the article will be through case example. These concepts offer an expanded view of a client's presenting problem. Just as changing to a wide angle lens on a camera offers a different perspective, making possible different photos, so too, the three generational view of a situation offers a greater number of pictures or assessments.

A recovering 40 year old gay man surviving the deaths of former lovers and friends during the AIDS epidemic serves as an example of the usefulness of widening the lens. It was particularly

Dava L. Weinstein is in private practice in New York City.

difficult for this man to accept that these persons were really dead. Widening the picture to include how his family dealt with death provided direction for clinical intervention. His family had no rituals to mark death: no funerals, no visits to grave sites of deceased members, no marking of the anniversary of deaths. The clinical intervention was to educate this individual to the universal need for ritual in response to death and discuss with him that his family was "under ritualized" (Imber-Black, Roberts & Whiting, 1988). The client was urged to develop his own meaningful rituals to mark the losses of loved ones. This work was put in the context of necessary growth in recovery. Taking a family history of attitudes towards and responses to death enlarged the view of the client's experience thus facilitating the above intervention.

Some of the common misconceptions about lesbians and gay men concerning their families are that they purposely distance themselves from their families of origin, that their families of origin do not want to have anything to do with them, that they are not interested in creating family life, that they have no interest in parenting, that they do not have children, that they have no relationship to a religious organization such as church or synagogue, that same sex relationships do not last, and that they isolate themselves in geographic pockets and do not participate in community life. All these and other embedded myths of our society influence the clinician's thinking about homosexual clients.

The three generational view does much to counter these myths that lead one to think of persons who are members of a sexual minority group in a very one dimensional way devoid of a family context. An additional case example supporting the need to elicit family of origin information is a 32 year old lesbian who had made repeated efforts (through AA and formal treatment) at sobriety. In taking a family history it became clear that she felt that her relationship with her family would be lost if she stayed sober. When sober she was confronted with her sexual orientation and bewildered by it. She struggled with the question of informing her family only during periods of abstinence. She also experienced intense panic that her family would disown her if they learned she was a lesbian. It was only when family members were discussed individually that she could begin to identify allies who would support both her recovery and her sexual orientation.

Fortunately, the perpetuation of misinformation via myths is changing. The 1990 federal census, in which one was able to indicate a common law relationship and the gender of that partner was a boon for all Americans living in arrangements other than heterosexual marriage contracts. The addictions literature is devoting articles and journal issues to treating lesbians and gay men, and there is a body of professional literature addressing the mental health needs of lesbians and gay men as a special population (see Finnegan & McNally, 1987; Kus, 1990; Shernoff & Scott, 1988; Silverstein, 1990).

Certainly there has been an increase in the professional literature addressing aspects of lesbian/gay relationships and family life. In the family therapy field the January/February 1991 issue of *The Family Therapy Networker* ran its cover story: "Gays and Lesbians Are Out of the Closet. Are Therapists Still In the Dark?" Other examples include the *Journal of Homosexuality*'s special issue on "Homosexuality and the Family" (Bozett, 1989); Shernoff and Finnegan's (1991) article on family treatment with chemically dependent lesbians and gay men; Slater and Mencher's work (1991) on the lesbian life cycle; Bozett's (1990) discourse on gay fathers; and Goodman's work (1990) on lesbian mothers.

There is, however, a gap in the literature. Until recently, adult homosexual men and women in relationship to their families of origin were not discussed frequently. Exceptions were articles on psychosocial issues of gay men with AIDS (Keeper, 1988); teens' and young adults' responses from their families about their homosexuality (Heron, 1983); and Weston's anthropological study of members of the San Francisco area gay/lesbian community (1991). There is a need to incorporate family three generational thinking into the discussion of treatment of lesbians and gay men, specifically those struggling with addictions.

USE OF THE GENOGRAM TO GATHER INFORMATION AND IDENTIFY FAMILY THEMES

The genogram (McGoldrick & Gerson, 1985) is a method of diagraming family members. The first step in gathering information in a three (or more) generational format is to ask for the names, relationships and ages of family members (living and deceased). This includes separations, divorces, remarriages and adoptions, still births, miscarriages and abortions. This becomes the bones, the skeleton, of the genogram. An additional piece of basic, skeletal, information is who lives with whom. This can be indicated by drawing lines around living units.

The clinician needs to develop a response to clients who insist they are sufficiently cut off from their family that family of origin information is irrelevant. These clients need to be given a reason for collecting this information. More often than not a straightforward explanation will do: that the information about their family (or families in the situation of couples) will give the clinician a context in which to understand their experience of the world now.

Any idea can be developed into a theme through questioning with responses being recorded on the genogram. These ideas include, but are not limited to, the nature of the relationships between family members (i.e., close, distant, cut off, etc.; see McGoldrick & Gerson, 1985 for instructions on how to diagram relationships), religious affiliation of individual members, sexual orientation, physical illness, drug or alcohol abuse or recovery, cause of death of deceased members, level of education of all family members, or type of employment and so on. The kinds of information to gather are endless. Certainly for the same-sex oriented individual noting who in the family also has a minority sexual orientation or who in the family that individual feels could have been lesbian or gay in another context is very informative. Equally important in addictive situations is the history of who takes care of whom either financially or emotionally,

Using themes culled from the genogram can be very effective. For example, consider the woman who had made repeated efforts at abstinence. She plotted the health of family members on her genogram. There were three generations of women with breast cancer. She was also of an age where her friendship network included women who had breast cancer. She had never discussed her family medical history before or her tremendous fear for her own health. Each time she scheduled a mammography during a period of abstinence she would relapse. Identifying the theme in her family of breast cancer together with the pattern of her relapses focused her treatment.

In the above example a theme flowed from the extensive history of breast cancer seen on the genogram to an understanding of the present pattern of relapses. The information can flow in the opposite direction as well from present back in time to historical experiences. "Let's look at the genogram again. Where did you get the idea that intimacy always involves a third person? . . . the idea that every person who is an adult must drink? . . . the idea that the world is a dangerous place and even your lover is not trustworthy? . . . where in your family of origin did you observe this? . . . did anyone in your extended family do it differently?" Referring to the identified problem behavior as "an idea" indirectly introduces "the idea" of different possible realities. After all, it is *just* an idea.

Figure 1 is an example of a diagram of a family in which three out of four grandparents are deceased and the identified patient is a lesbian middle sibling. The genogram includes aunts and uncles, cousins', marriages and children. The client is distinguished by two concentric circles (or a square within a square if the client is male). The words "alc." or "drugs" indicate who in the extended family has alcohol or drug problems. Circles represent females and squares males. Solid lines connecting individuals horizontally indicate marriages and dashed horizontal lines indicate intimate relationships without marriage. Same sex committed relationships denied the benefit of legal marriage are indicated with a solid line. Divorce is indicated with two short lines drawn perpendicular to the horizontal marriage connection. Separation is indicated with one short line perpendicular to the horizontal marriage connection. Lines indicating offspring connect parents with children listed beneath the parents. Deaths are represented by an "x." If a couple were being treated, the genogram would include each individual's family of origin (see McGoldrick & Gerson 1985 for guidance in plotting out more complicated genograms).

Creating the genogram in the counseling session is a clinical intervention in and of itself. It organizes the client's family history as the client provides the information. The clinician can simply explain the symbols used as the genogram evolves. The woman constructing the above genogram began to recognize, to literally "see," a family theme that no one in her family who was a substance abuser had ever stopped using alcohol or drugs. This realization provided the context for reframing the client as a "pio-

Figure 1

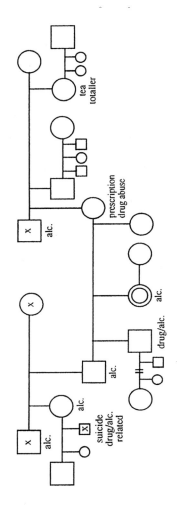

neer." Not only was she forging ahead in her life as different from her family because she was the only lesbian, she was also pioneering for her family as the only member who was abstaining from alcohol and drugs. No wonder she felt different from her family–she was! "Pioneer" has a positive ring to it crediting her with the strength it takes to be different from one's family of origin.

The above case illustrates a series of questions uniformly asked of gay men and lesbians with drug or alcohol problems. Who in the family knows of their sexual orientation or, where applicable, their struggle with their sexual identity? Who in the family is aware of their drug or alcohol problem? Are there any drug or alcohol problems in the family? Responses are noted on the genogram. It is a very efficient way to determine how open individuals are about their sexuality or their drinking/drugging history and efforts at abstinence. It is noteworthy that some families experience a member's abstinence from alcohol or drugs as more toxic than that family member's homosexuality.

This line of questioning determines the level of secrecy in a family. Is this level of secrecy an impediment to recovery for the individual? When does the clinician push the client to disclose his/her homosexuality? When is information withheld a secret and when is it maintaining privacy? The Alcoholics Anonymous (AA) slogan, "You are only as sick as your secrets" provides some guidance in this clinical question. What is the client's reasoning for not "coming out" to family? If the secret is based in internalized homophobia experienced as self loathing and shame, it is indeed a sick secret.

The case example of Mr. S., a 55 year old gay male estranged from his family, is illustrative of the struggle with secrecy. He was referred for individual counseling by his internist when he was eight months sober and very much involved in AA. He was extremely anxious about being HIV positive (see Figure 2).

The locations of various siblings were placed on the genogram. Specific questions about the frequency of contact with siblings revealed minimal connection with family of origin throughout Mr. S.'s adult life. Note that his youngest brother is also gay and has raised two foster children with his life partner. During his childhood his family had been very active in their small Baptist community.

Figure 2

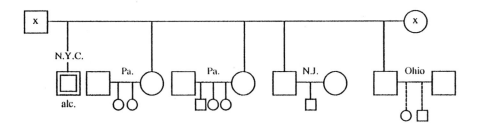

Note: dotted vertical lines indicate foster children.

When he moved away to go to college he began a life of compartmentalized experiences. His family had no idea of his gay life experience in a large urban setting. Mr. S. organized his life in response to internal and external homophobia. He lived two very separate lives. He was a confirmed bachelor, affable high school teacher who was invited to all the social events of his colleagues and the secretive individual whose sole experience as a gay man was anonymous sex in public places. His life was full of fear, shame and emotional isolation and pain. He confronted his alcoholism and joined AA when controlled drinking in social situations crossed the line and his behavior became disruptive when he socialized.

His isolation was particularly poignant in light of having a younger brother who was gay, open with the family, living in a long term relationship and raising foster children. The genogram was the vehicle for talking about his siblings (both parents were deceased) and for realizing that, judging from the relationship the younger brother had with them, they would probably be open to learning of Mr. S's homosexuality. The hope was that his family could be supportive of Mr. S. if he became sick. The AA experience of observing "straight" meeting members reaching out to gay members also helped in his decision to take the risk to tell his siblings he was gay, HIV positive, and in recovery. He did this by calling all his siblings from the counselor's office. Their responses to him went a long way towards combating the tremendous shame and isolation he had been living with his entire adult life. The genogram facilitated this work, making it happen more quickly. Time was of the essence. Mr. S. died due to AIDS-related illness shortly after reconnecting with his family. He had effectively created a supportive loving circle which was there for him in the hospital, including family visits and AA meetings brought to his bedside.

Steven, a 28 year old gay man referred for counseling by his employee assistance program, provides a third illustration of the use of the genogram. He had just completed a residential rehabilitation program. Job jeopardy was the motivation for going to treatment and agreeing to the aftercare plan. The extent of Steven's illness (i.e., excessive blackouts, inability to perform the most basic activities of daily living) prior to drinking cessation left him on shaky ground in early recovery. He was also struggling to leave his lover of five years. The men occupied the second story of a two family house owned by the non-alcoholic lover, Paul. Paul was a stereotypic example of a caretaker. He had done everything for his very sick alcoholic partner ranging from all the household chores to cleaning up Steven's vomit. In contrast to the unending care he provided, Paul was unwilling to be involved in any counseling sessions individually or with Steven.

It became clear to Steven that Paul was getting increasingly irritable and bossy towards him. The relationship worked well prior to Steven's abstinence. This included the two men spending all holidays downstairs with Paul's large extended Italian family. Paul's family accepted his homosexuality as long as he remained under their roof. However, with Steven's recovery and his ability to begin to make even the simplest day to day decisions for himself, the couple's relationship within the context of Paul's extended family began to breakdown. Note that the line around a subset on the genogram marks a living unit (see Figure 3).

The first sessions with Steven were spent creating his family genogram. Steven's family drinking history was generations long. The theme that quickly emerged was that Steven's life consisted of one alcohol-related loss after another. Steven readily accepted that

150

Figure 3

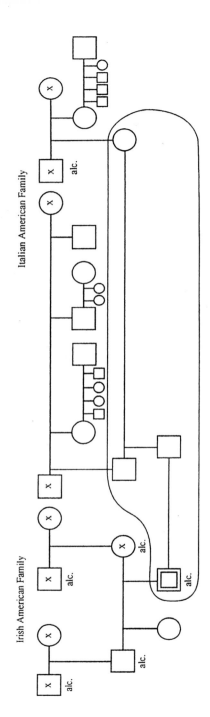

Irish American Family

Italian American Family

formulation of his experience dating back to early childhood. The genogram highlighted the emerging theme of his track record for surviving losses. From the idea of "track record" a metaphor for growth in recovery evolved: that Steven was in training, learning something new, practicing. The three generational perspective gave this reframe its power. He was indeed a top rate athlete when it came to the stamina required for "long distance running." This frame of his reality made it possible for him to come to peace with his plan to leave his lover. This was another loss due to alcohol. It was recognized as a healthy loss of a relationship that could only exist while Steven was drinking and his stamina as an athlete in training would help him survive it.

REFRAMING

The case examples above also illustrate reframing (Watzlawick, Weakland & Fisch, 1974). Reframing is used to create a different reality than the client's. Creating a different reality causes a very important shift in the presenting problem. Defining a different problem increases the number of possible solutions. An example of this is the 48 year old lesbian recovering alcoholic who began to feel guilty about not phoning her mother after a certain period of time had passed since the previous call. The situation was compounded when she then became immobilized by the guilt. The reframe was that perhaps the feeling she was calling "guilt" was her own internal signalling system telling her it was time to call her mother. This seemingly simplistic reframe freed the client of the stagnating feeling of guilt and allowed her to practice initiating preplanned phone contact with her mother as a way of being in control of her own life.

When the woman in the earlier case illustration was told she is a pioneer her status as lesbian and recovering alcoholic was being defined positively by reframing. "Pioneer" has a positive quality in our culture which facilitated a different experience for her with her family. In Steven's situation reframing dealing with loss in recovery as training for the sport of long distance running supported his strength.

RESTRAINING CHANGE

The strategic technique of asking clients to carefully consider the consequences of any sought after change (Watzlawick, Weakland & Fisch, 1974) before working to achieve it is an effective method of anticipating pulls against change. The individual, couple, or family's genogram and their listing of significant persons in their present environment provide guidelines for counseling the client through this process. How would change affect these relationships? Restraining change is particularly helpful when the client system has had more than one unsuccessful formal treatment attempt at righting the situation (Weinstein, 1985). The clinician's cautionary attitude puts the responsibility for change squarely in the hands of the client.

Restraining change can be introduced through the following task of listing positive and negative consequences, the pros and cons of achieving the desired change. "Before doing anything to actually achieve your goal it is important to realize the advantages and disadvantages of reaching it." These lists include the effects change would have on interpersonal relationships. For those persons with a working knowledge of AA, the counselor may add that this list making is a variation on the AA slogan "Be careful what you pray for." If a person cannot think of any negative consequence, the counselor can help the client begin the list making by offering one on the positive side and one on the negative side.

A lesbian couple who had been living together for seven years requested couples treatment for their constant arguing. They were both recovering from addictions. Disagreeing about the extent to which they should be out to family and work colleagues was just one of their many arguments. Both women had had extensive counseling prior to and in recovery, and both women had a clear understanding of the emotional deprivation and abandonment they had experienced in their childhoods. When one partner was age eleven, her mother committed suicide; when the other partner was age eight, her mother abandoned the family. Their experience of the constant threat of abandonment was similar and punctuated their fights. Their fighting seemed to be a powerful way to reassure each of them that the other was there.

The presenting problem, basic family genograms for both, and ascertaining the extent of their social network's involvement in the problem were established in the initial interviews (see Weber, McKeever & McDaniel, 1985 for a discussion of the initial interview). The couple was given the task, in between sessions, to think of all the consequences of reaching their goal of not fighting as much as they did. They might or might not compare their lists before the next joint appointment. This couple returned with similar items on their positive consequence lists: less tension at home, easier time making social plans, more closeness and trust, more love making, etc. Neither one was able to come up with any negative consequences of diminished fighting.

Circular questioning (Nelson, Fleuridas & Rosenthal, 1986; Penn, 1982) is an effective way to help clients develop a list of negative consequences of reaching a sought after goal. This type of questioning addresses the impact change will have on relationships in the client system: if your fighting diminished, who amongst your friends or family would be most upset? Who would be most happy for you? Who among your friends would miss talking about your problems the most? How would the change affect friendships? These are questions asked about third parties not present. Also the questioning can highlight the negative consequences of increased closeness between members of the couple or family grouping: Which of you would miss the fighting most? Which of you might be bored without the fighting? What would you devise as a way to feel intensely connected? These questions lead to the development of a list of negative consequences of change including but not limited to the loss of a powerful connection, possible boredom, the possibility that the couple or one member of the couple would realize they do not want to be in the relationship, or the possibility of greater intimacy. The clinician can explore answers to questions referring to the couple's genograms and their friendship network.

Couples with the historical experiences of abuse and neglect are able to see the negative aspects of intimacy. Their lists may include such statements as "fear of intimacy . . . the more you have, the more you lose . . . I feel smothered, captured . . . I lose myself . . . I'll never be able to get out . . . I'll have to take what she wants to do into account when making plans . . . I'll lose my freedom to do what ever I want when ever I want . . . I'll have to be monogamous'' and so on. As the lists of the pros and cons of reaching a sought-after goal evolve, the counselor can "walk around resistance" (Erickson, 1979), challenging the couple to seriously consider their plan for change and all its ramifications.

In the case example of this lesbian couple the task of considering the consequences of change led them to the realization that they knew no other way to relate. They did not have the foggiest idea of what life would be like with diminished fighting. This became clear when they had tremendous difficulty coming up with any negatives of diminished fighting prior to the circular questioning which focused them on loss and fear. They became allies in researching possible ways to relate if their fighting were to diminish. They were given the task of exploring alternate ways to be a couple by observing couples they knew and then discussing together the pattern they saw. They also "interviewed" those couples whom they were close enough to about each individual couple's way of relating.

CONCLUSION

The family therapy field offers the addictions specialist working with lesbians and gay men a way to organize one's thinking which includes family of origin and family of choice networks. As the case examples in this article illustrate, an expanded view of a client's family history and connections facilitates treatment. It allows for the assessment of a presenting problem in a context. The fuller the assessment, the more opportunity for clinical interventions of reframing, recognizing themes or restraining change.

REFERENCES

Bozett, F. (1990). Fathers who are gay. In R. Kus (Ed.). *Keys to Caring. Assisting Gay and Lesbian Clients* (pp. 106-118). Boston: Alyson Publications.
Carter, B., & McGoldrick, M. (Eds.). (1989). *The changing family life cycle. A framework for family therapy* (2nd ed.). Boston: Allyn & Bacon.
Fisch, R., Weakland, J., & Segal, L. (1982). *The tactics of change. Doing therapy briefly*. Washington: Jossey-Bass Inc., Publishers.

Goodman, B. (1990). Lesbian mothers. In R. Kus (Ed.). *Keys to caring. Assisting gay and lesbian clients* (pp. 119-124). Boston: Alyson Publications.

Heron, A. (Ed.). (1983). *One teenager in ten. Writings by gay and lesbian youth.* Boston: Alyson Publications.

Kus, R. (Ed.). (1990). *Keys to caring. Assisting gay and lesbian clients.* Boston: Alyson Publications.

McGoldrick, M., & Gerson, R. (1985). *Genograms In family assessment.* New York: W.W. Norton & Co., Inc..

Nelson, T., Fleuridas, C. & Rosenthal, D. (1986). The evolution of circular questions: Training family therapists. *Journal of Marital and Family Therapy, 12,* 113-127.

Penn, P. (1982). Circular questioning. *Family Process, 12,* 267-280.

Shernoff, M., & Scott, W. (Eds.). (1988). *The sourcebook on lesbian/gay health care* (2nd ed.). Washington: National Lesbian/Gay Health Foundation.

Slater, S., & Mencher, J. (1991). The lesbian life cycle: A contextual approach. *American Journal of Orthopsychiatry, 61,* 372-382.

Watzlawick, P., Weakland, J., & Fisch, R. (1974). *Change. Principles of problem formation and problem resolution.* New York: W.W. Norton & Co., Inc.

Weber, T., McKeever, J., & McDaniel, S. (1985). A beginner's guide to the problem-oriented first family interview. *Family Process, 24,* 357-364.

Weston, K. (1991). *Families we choose.* New York: Columbia University Press.